# A Story A Day

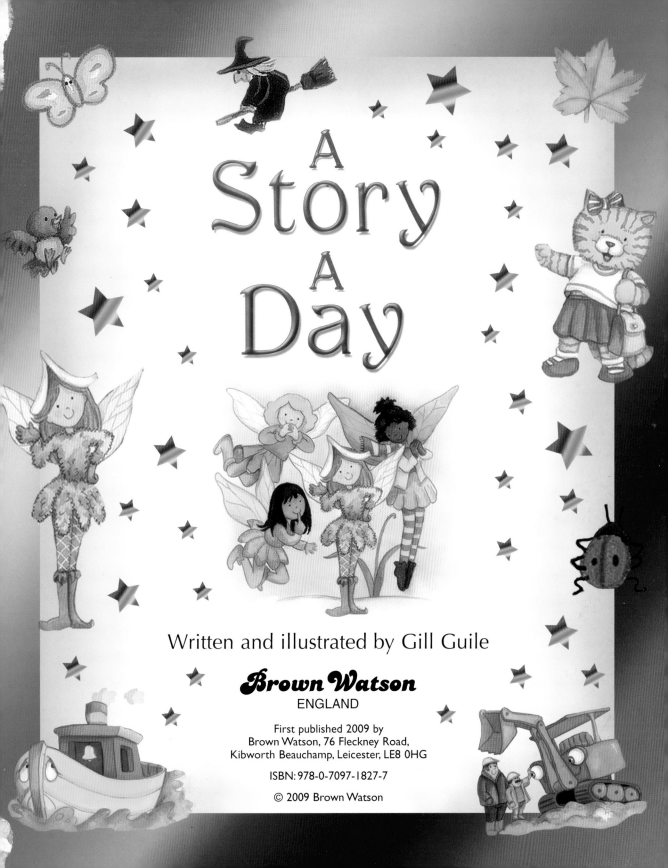

# A Story A Day

Written and illustrated by Gill Guile

## Brown Watson
ENGLAND

First published 2009 by
Brown Watson, 76 Fleckney Road,
Kibworth Beauchamp, Leicester, LE8 0HG

ISBN: 978-0-7097-1827-7

 **1 January**

## New Year's Day

Last night Tom and Lauren's family had a wonderful New Year's Eve, with two other families.

The guests left after midnight, but Tom and Lauren have made a pact with their friends to stay awake all night and meet in the garden at nine o'clock. It's getting very hard to stay awake now. Mummy peeps in, 'I'm not leaving until you're sleeping,' she tells them.

They close their eyes and pretend to sleep. When he next opens his eyes, Tom is astonished to find it is eight o'clock! He's cross with himself for not staying awake, until he looks out of the window and sees everything blanketed in snow. 'Wake up, Lauren,' he shouts. 'We can build a snowman!'

After breakfast they go outside. Nine o'clock comes and goes but there's no sign of the others. Can you guess why? Their friends stayed awake all night and now they are too tired to play, but Tom and Lauren had a lovely time. I think they're quite pleased they fell asleep, don't you?

# 2 January

## The Snowman

Tom and Lauren build a really cool snowman, but it's very sunny and the snowman starts to melt! His carrot nose droops and one button eye slowly slips down his face. The line of acorns, making up his smile, glides downwards, making him look rather sad. And he is sad, because tomorrow he might disappear altogether! 'Not long to go now,' he says to the little robin. 'Oh don't worry,' says the robin as he flies away.

 # 3 January

When the robin returns half an hour later, the snowman has only one button eye left and his carrot nose is on the grass. 'I don't think I'll be here next time you come,' he says. 'I said don't worry,' the robin replies and flies away once again. Then as the second button bounces to the ground, the snowman feels something soft and cold falling on his face. It's snowing again!

### Epiphany

Over two thousand years ago, when Jesus Christ, the Son of God, was born, a new star rose in the sky from the east. Three wise men saw this mysterious star and they knew it was a sign from God, which would guide them to the place where baby Jesus was to be born. These men were also kings and their names were Caspar, Melchior and Balthazar.

## 4 January

Soon everywhere is covered in snow once more and the snowman can hear Tom and Lauren coming back into the garden. They start to remake him and this time he has gloves, a scarf and holly for his cap. Finally, they put back his little button eyes and the first thing the snowman sees is the little robin, watching him from a tree.

'I told you not to worry,' he says. 'Now you look even better than you did before!'

## The Thief

It's back to school today and the twins can't wait to see all their friends again, after the school holidays.

Soon it's playtime and everyone rushes into the playground to make a pile of snowballs. Before long there is a large stack of snowballs in one corner of the yard, and an even bigger one at the opposite side.

The twins organise everyone into teams, but before they can start the snowball fight, Mr Fraser, the headmaster, calls them over. Snowball fights are banned in case someone gets hurt.

# 6 January

Each carried a gift for the infant; they brought gold, frankincense and myrrh. The wise men followed the star until it led them to a humble stable, in Bethlehem. Inside they found baby Jesus lying in a manger, surrounded by Mary and Joseph, and all the animals that shared the stable. Epiphany is the name given to the day the three kings gave their gifts to Jesus, and in some countries it is the day children receive their Christmas gifts.

# 8 January

The children are very disappointed, but they abandon the game and decide to kick a football around instead. Just before playtime ends, the twins hear the headmaster shouting: 'Stop, thief! He's got my bike!'

A man has managed to unlock Mr Fraser's bicycle and is pedalling furiously across the playground towards the exit. 'Get to the snowballs,' shouts one of the twins.

# 9 January

The children race over to the piles of snowballs and hurl them at the thief. The bombardment of snow knocks him off his bicycle, but he quickly escapes through the school gates on foot, leaving Mr Fraser's new bicycle behind.

Mr Fraser is delighted with the children's quick thinking and reconsiders his snowball ban. On one side of the playground he sets up a range of targets for the children to aim at. That way, everyone is happy, especially Mr Fraser who won't have to walk home after all!

# 11 January

Today things have changed. After waving goodbye to Lucy, Mummy takes Benji on a different walk. They turn into the village and Mummy ties Benji up outside the supermarket. She's inside for a long time and comes out carrying lots of shopping. They travel home on a bus, which is very exciting for Benji because he has to have a ticket too, although he's not allowed on the seats! Back home, Benji wonders what's going on.

# 10 January

## The Big Surprise

Benji is Lucy's special friend. He likes to follow her everywhere. Every day he helps Mummy walk Lucy to school. They have a long walk back home, across the fields and through the woods. Then he waits patiently for three o'clock, when school finishes and he can meet Lucy at the school gates. This is the best time of the day for the little puppy.

## 12 January

Benji only gets a short walk because Mummy has a very busy day ahead. Benji has found a balloon bobbing around in the hallway, so he chases it round the house. As he races into Mummy and Daddy's bedroom, he notices lots of brightly wrapped presents piled on the bed. He leaps after the balloon and knocks it downstairs and under the table, which is set with party hats, slices of pizza, buns, crisps and a huge chocolate cake with five candles.

## 13 January

It doesn't look like Benji will be collecting Lucy today. Six of her friends are waiting in the house with arms full of balloons. Daddy's car turns into the driveway and Mummy asks everyone to be quiet. As Lucy walks through the door the children shower her with balloons and streamers and shout, 'Happy Birthday' to her. Lucy loves her surprise party and Benji has a wonderful time.

# 14 January

## A Bedtime Story

Daddy tucks David up in bed and reads him a bedtime story. Outside, snow and hail batter the window but inside, David is wrapped up tightly in his duvet feeling snug and warm.

The story David chooses is about a koala bear who lives in Australia, which is about as far away from Britain as you can imagine. When it is Winter in Europe, it is Summer in many countries like Australia, South America and parts of Africa.

# 15 January

## The Forgetful Koala

Kelly Koala is always in trouble because she finds it so hard to remember things.

She forgets to tell Mummy when she goes out to play, she forgets to put her watch on, she forgets her school lunch and her homework. Sometimes she even forgets to go to school!

Every morning when she gets out of bed, Kelly knows she is going to forget something important but she doesn't know what to do about it.

# 16 January

Katie Kangaroo feels very sorry for Kelly and tries to think of a way to help her remember the most important things.

She finds a little notepad and pencil in a cupboard at home and takes it round to Kelly's house. Now Kelly can write everything down that she has to remember. 'What a good idea,' thinks Kelly. But she's so absent minded that she keeps forgetting where she's put the notepad!

# 17 January

Katie thinks this is really funny because there is an absolutely perfect place for Kelly to keep her pad and pencil. Like Katie and lots of other Australian animals, Kelly is a marsupial.

Female marsupials have a little pouch or pocket near their tummies. This is where the mummies keep their babies when they are small and it is the perfect place for Kelly to keep her notepad. She hardly forgets anything now!

# 18 January

## A Bad Spell

In the jungle, the animals are playing Blind Man's Bluff, while Little Fairy is fluttering in and out of the trees. What is she looking for? Monkey knows, because he found it earlier this morning. It is a book of very magical spells and, being naughty, he has decided to try one of the spells out on his friends.

The animals blindfold Lion. He has to catch them and guess who each of them is. EASY!

# 19 January

Elephant has flappy ears and a long trunk; Giraffe is tall with a long neck; and Tortoise is so slow!

Then monkey casts his spell:
'Your shapes I'll change
to something strange.
That flappy ear will disappear,
And what came last
will now be fast!'

Lion catches the first animal. It seems to have small ears, a tiny nose and wrinkly skin. Who can it be?

The second animal is impossible to catch because it's moving too fast! Who can this be?

# 20 January

Lion is very confused and takes off his blindfold to see what is happening. All his friends have changed shape. Behind them, high up in the banana tree, he can see Monkey laughing so hard that he nearly loses his balance! Lion opens his mouth to roar at Monkey but all that comes out is a tiny squeak!

Little Fairy sees Monkey clutching her spell book and realises what he's done. She is very cross and grabs the book from Monkey.

# 21 January

'Hear my spell you naughty ape,
I'll turn you yellow,
And change your shape.
You must be good
and stop being bad,
Or my spell will last
and you'll be sad!'

In a puff of pink smoke, they all change back, except for Monkey who has suddenly changed into a giant banana! He feels very foolish. The spell will wear off by bedtime, but every time he is naughty he will turn back into a big yellow banana! I think he will be a very good monkey from now on, don't you?

 **22 January**

## The Art Lesson

Today at school, the children are having an art lesson with Mrs Harper. This is Elliott's favourite day, because he's rather good at drawing and painting, and he'd love to be an artist when he grows up. Today Mrs Harper is having a competition to see who paints the best picture of an Australian creature. It can be a bird, fish, insect or animal.

**23 January**

Mrs Harper lays out a huge pile of photographs for the children to choose from. Nicki likes a colourful, red and yellow parrot; Chris wants to draw a big, fierce-looking shark; Beth picks a kangaroo with a long tail and powerful legs; and Vicki thinks it would be fun to paint a kookaburra. But Elliott just can't make up his mind. There are so many to choose from.

# 24 January

Elliott doesn't want the pretty pink flamingo, the cute budgerigar, or the cuddly koala, he wants something which will catch the teacher's eye. Finally, he finds the perfect creature, it's a very scary looking crocodile. He decides to paint the crocodile swimming in the water, with it's huge mouth open wide, showing rows of sharp, pointed teeth. The children take the photographs back to their desks and collect paper, brushes and paint pots.

# 25 January

Mrs Harper is very pleased with the children's paintings and hangs them all around the classroom. It's difficult for her to pick the winning picture because they are all so good. But then she comes to Elliott's painting and it is the best by far. Mrs Harper gives first prize to Elliott. He wins a big bag of sweets, which he happily shares with all his classmates at break time.

# 26 January

## Little Lost Zebra

Little Zebra is lost. He cannot find his mummy and there is no one else around. He begins to worry. There are three paths in front of him, but which is the way back home?

It is very hot so he follows the first track down to the river to have a drink. As he leans forward, a fearsome green head with rows of sharp white teeth explodes out of the water! Little Zebra is terrified and bolts back to the clearing.

# 27 January

Behind him, Crocodile climbs out of the water and shakes himself dry. 'Maybe the second path is safer,' thinks Little Zebra. But as he trots along he hears a faint drumming sound. The noise gets closer and louder until the trees begin to shake and the ground trembles!

Then a huge, grey monster with flapping ears thunders across his path! Little Zebra races back to the clearing once more.

# 28 January

Behind him, Elephant crashes around in the bushes.

'This third path must be the way home,' sobs Little Zebra rushing along.

He stops suddenly as he hears a terrible roar. It is so loud that it makes his ears ring and his legs shake, so he gallops back as fast as he can.

'He's over here!' shouts Lion.

'He's in the clearing.' Little Zebra is very scared.

# 29 January

He can hear the green sharp-toothed monster splashing up the first path. And the frightening ground-shaking monster is thundering up the second path. And the loud, hairy howling monster is roaring up the third path! HELP!

Then something lifts him high into the air. He squeezes his eyes shut and wishes Mummy was there but it's only Elephant with Crocodile and Lion!

Tired Little Zebra rides on Old Elephant's back all the way home to his mummy. What an exciting day!

# 30 January

## The Tooth Fairy

Have you ever heard of the Tooth Fairy? She's a tiny little creature, about the size of your thumb, and when children's teeth fall out, the Tooth Fairy collects them. The next time you lose a tooth, put it under your pillow when you go to bed, and leave a little note with it. If you are lucky, the Tooth Fairy will take the tooth and leave a coin in its place.

# 31 January

The Tooth Fairy has to work very hard because there are hundreds of teeth to collect every night. She takes them back to a magic land where all the fairy folk live. They use the teeth to build beautiful castles and palaces for the Fairy King and Queen. But the Tooth Fairy doesn't like bad teeth, she only picks clean, white baby teeth which fall out by themselves. So don't forget to clean your teeth every day until they sparkle.

 # 1 February

## Spiky Solutions

Holly Hedgehog wakes up one sunny winter's day and pokes her head out of the crisp pile of leaves she has been sleeping under. Holly has been asleep for two whole months now, although some years she sleeps for even longer. It is unusual for Holly to be awake during the day, but she thinks it might be nice to stretch her legs and go for a stroll!

# 2 February

On her way across the garden, Holly spots Ricky Robin flitting to and fro with scraps of bread and bacon rind in his beak. He is busy collecting food for a party at the oak tree, which starts at one o'clock, but it is already five minutes to one and Ricky is worried that his friends will arrive before he is ready. He can only carry one scrap of food in his beak on each journey and Holly notices that he is very tired. Then she thinks of a clever way to help.

 # 3 February

She curls up into a spiky ball and rolls around the lawn. All the bits of food stick to her prickles. She does look funny!

Holly collects all the food and trots across the grass to the oak tree just as the guests are arriving. Martha Mouse and Scarlet Squirrel have come together. Belinda Bluebird has flown, and Cyril Snail finally slithers across the garden slowly. Ricky Robin is delighted and invites Holly to join them.

# 4 February

Holly has a lovely afternoon with all her friends, but as the sun begins to sink in the sky, it becomes cold again. Holly suddenly feels sleepy, so she says goodbye to everyone and shuffles back across the lawn to her cosy nest of leaves. As the last leaf settles over her head, Holly gives a gentle snore. She is already fast asleep! What a wonderful day she has had!

# 5 February

## Wendy's Wood

Wendy looks out of her bedroom window and straight into the wood at the bottom of the garden. All the leaves have fallen during winter, so it's difficult for Wendy to recognise all the different tree types. Her big brother, William, says there are lots of clues in the wood and offers to help. Wendy thinks this could be fun and runs off to find her wellies. William tells Wendy to look for an oak tree first.

# 6 February

Wendy knows acorns come from oak trees, so she looks high up in the trees for squirrels, which eat acorns. She soon spots a couple and follows them to a sturdy tree with a dark, rough trunk. Under the tree are old dried leaves. 'Found one!' she laughs. Wendy pops a leaf in her pocket. Next she looks for old conkers, which are the fruit of the horse chestnut tree. She often plays conkers with her friends so she should easily recognise this tree.

 ## 7 February

William says horse chestnut leaves have five to seven fingers. She soon spots one, and pockets a leaf, then she rushes off to find a sycamore. They have squarish leaves with three to seven fat fingers. William says sycamores have smooth tree bark and seeds like helicopters! When Wendy finds a seed, she drops it and watches as it spins slowly down. The silver birch is easy to spot because of its white bark. The holly tree is easy too, with its Christmassy, green prickly leaf.

 ## 8 February

Soon, Wendy's pockets are bulging with dried leaves. When she gets home she traces round the leaves and labels each picture. Then she sticks them in a scrapbook, ready to take to school on Monday. William thinks Wendy's teacher would like to see the scrapbook. The teacher thinks the book is wonderful and gives Wendy a gold star! Later the children are taken on a nature ramble and have fun making their own leaf scrapbooks. Why don't you try it?

 ## 9 February

### Sally Spider

Sally Spider lives in the wood, half way up a sycamore tree, with lots of spider friends.

Each day they make new webs by spinning and weaving threads of silk into wonderful webs. Spiders live in their webs but they are also sticky traps for flies, which is how spiders catch their food.

 ## 10 February

Sally is a very quick weaver, so she usually finishes her web by lunchtime and then has nothing else to do for the rest of the day. In summer there are lots of other creatures around to chat to, but in chilly February everyone comes out of their burrows and nests just long enough to find some food, then they rush back to their warm homes.

## 11 February

Sally thinks that if she could keep her friends warm, they might stay around for a chat. She knows exactly what to do. All afternoon she spins and weaves until she has a pile of long, thin webs. The other spiders are puzzled because these are the strangest webs they've ever seen! 'Whatever is she up to?' they wonder. The next day they find out.

## 12 February

When Ruby Robin flies past, Sally calls out to her. 'Would you like a nice warm scarf, Ruby?'

Ruby is delighted and chats for ages! A little later, Henry Hare hops by and Sally asks, 'Would you like a nice warm scarf, Henry?'

Henry is so pleased, he stays until teatime. Everybody wants a scarf. So Sally is never bored, she spins and chats all day long!

# 13 February

## Valentine's Day

Tomorrow is Valentine's Day and Jack is making a card for a very special person. He draws a big red heart on the front of his card and fills the space inside with kisses. Jack doesn't sign it because Valentine's cards are usually sent in secret and it's fun trying to guess who they are from. Jack leaves the card on the very special person's doormat.

# 14 February

The next morning, the very special person finds the card. She knows it's for her because it says 'To Mummy' on the envelope! Tucked inside is an orange lollipop. Mummy laughs with delight and runs upstairs to give Jack a big hug. 'But how do you know it's from me?' Jack asks.

'Just a lucky guess,' laughs Mummy, hiding the envelope in her dressing gown pocket!

# 15 February

## No Place Like Home

There are some creatures that love snow, and the colder it gets, the better they like it.

Peggy Penguin lives in the Antarctic, which is down at the bottom of the world and a very chilly place to live. Everywhere is white and covered in snow. It is always Winter here.

Peggy lives on an iceberg in the sea with a large group of other penguins. Every day they swim and catch fish in the freezing waters.

# 16 February

Every few weeks, large ships, bulging with tourists, stop at Peggy's iceberg to photograph the penguins. These people come from much hotter lands, which Peggy longs to visit, because she is tired of being cold. One day Peggy manages to stow away on a ship bound for Italy. She hides amongst boxes and crates until the boat finally docks.

The sun blazes fiercely over bright flowers, green trees, noisy people and smelly cars.

# 17 February

Peggy is hot, hungry and very homesick. Thoughts of the Antarctic fill her head and she longs for the cool, quiet calm of the iceberg. She scuttles back to her hiding place and waits for the ship to sail back south with new passengers. When she finally gets home, the penguins want to hear all about her travels. Peggy never dreams about other countries now because she knows, there's no place like home!

# 18 February

## The Scary Scarecrow

Mark, Victoria and Sophie are having a competition to see who can make the best scarecrow. Mark would love to win but he's only four and his eight year old twin sisters seem much smarter than him. They make their scarecrows in Farmer Ben's field, and Ben is going to give a prize for the best one.

Victoria has nearly finished. Her scarecrow has a lovely pink scarf and floppy hat, which she covers with bows and feathers.

# 19 February

Sophie's wears an old top hat, with matching gloves that she found in the dressing-up box. She has drawn a big smile on its pumpkin face. The two scarecrows look fabulous! Mark looks at his effort, an old brush with a scarf tied round it and decides to go home as he's sure he won't win. Back home he draws an angry face to show how he feels. He thinks it will make a good mask, but when he puts it on it scares the cat. This gives Mark an idea.

# 20 February

Mark races back to the field and ties his mask to the brush, just as Farmer Ben arrives. The farmer thinks the twins' scarecrows are great but he knows they won't scare the birds away, which is, of course, why we have scarecrows! So Mark's scary scarecrow wins the prize - a big bag of juicy apples, which he happily shares with his sisters. Then he goes home to draw another face. A happy smiley one this time!

## 21 February

### Bunny and Honey

Jamie has two cuddly pet rabbits, who live in the hut at the bottom of his garden. Bunny is a black and white rabbit. He is full of mischief and is always trying to escape. Honey is a large, gentle lop-eared rabbit, who just wants to be cuddled. Each morning before school, Jamie cleans out the rabbit hutch and gives them clean water and fresh food.

## 22 February

This morning Jamie hasn't closed the hutch door properly, so Bunny pushes it open with his nose and escapes into the garden. Jamie chases after him but it's too late, Bunny has disappeared. Mummy promises to help look for him after school, so Jamie locks Honey away and hopes Bunny doesn't get too cold outside.

Bunny is very pleased with himself. He nibbles some grass and then goes off to explore the garden.

## 23 February

As the day goes on, Bunny gets hungry and he remembers the juicy carrots and lettuce Jamie had brought that morning. He feels cold and he remembers the fresh warm hay in the hutch. He gets lonely, and worst of all he misses Honey. At four o'clock when Jamie gets home, the first thing he sees is a very unhappy rabbit, huddling next to the hutch. As Jamie opens the door, Bunny rushes in and snuggles next to Honey. Bunny has had his little adventure and he's quite happy to stay with Honey in future.

## 24 February

### Pancake Day

Pancake Day, or Shrove Tuesday, happens between the third and twenty-ninth of February each year. Traditionally, people used up all the foods they couldn't eat during Lent, like the butter and eggs in pancakes. Try them with syrup, or sugar and lemon. Delicious! In France, Pancake Day is 'Mardi Gras' (Fat Tuesday), and in Iceland it's called 'Bursting Day'. They must eat a lot of pancakes!

 ## 25 February

### Fashion Fairy

Little Fairy Lucy flutters round the snow blanketed garden. I wonder what she's looking for? She looks very pretty in her winter clothes. She's wearing a tiny pair of green gloves made out of moss; beautifully soft, mushroom-skin boots; cobweb tights and a winter heather dress. Her clothes keep her nice and warm but her head feels rather cold, so she's searching for a winter hat.

## 26 February

Most of the plants and trees in the garden have gone to sleep over winter. The holly bush looks fresh and bright with its red berries, but it would make a very prickly hat! She spots an acorn shell under the oak tree. It fits quite well, but Lucy suspects it probably looks a bit odd, and it keeps slipping over her eyes! Finally she sees the perfect hat, poking through the snow in the rockery. It's a snowdrop. When Lucy shows it to her friends, they all want one too!

 # 27 February

## The Roman Calendar

Before the modern calendar that we know today was invented, the month of February always had twenty-nine days. Ancient calendars also included only 10 months. Eventually two new months were added. The first was July, named after the famous Roman Emperor, Julius Caesar. This month has 31 days.

# 28 February

The second new month was August, named after another famous Roman Emperor, Augustus Caesar. This new month had only thirty days. One day less than July! Augustus wanted his month to be as long as Julius', so it is said that he pinched a day from February to make July and August equal, with thirty-one days each. So February became even shorter.

## 29 February

The moon takes approximately one month to travel round the earth. Most months last for thirty or thirty-one days. February is a rather unusual month, because every four years it has one extra day. We call this a Leap Year. Leap Years only occur when the number of years can be divided by the number four, as in 2004, 2008, 2012 and so on.

If you find it difficult to remember how many days there are in each month, you could try and learn this rhyme.

Thirty days has bright September, April, June, and dull November. All the rest have thirty-one, except for February alone, which has but twenty-eight days clear. Twenty-nine in each leap year.

# 1 March

## Rainy Day Puppets

It's raining today and Roseanna and Francesca are trying to think of something to do. Mummy asks them to look under their beds to see what they can find. Between them they discover three odd socks and an old black glove. The girls put their finds on the kitchen table, where Mummy has laid out felt tips, buttons, glue, scissors and some scraps of material. This looks interesting, the girls think.

# 2 March

Mummy helps the girls to sew on button eyes and draw noses and mouths on the socks. Then using the glue, they stick multicoloured strips on them to make hair. The hand puppets look really cool, and they can't wait to show them to their friends.

'But what shall we make with this old glove?' asks Roseanna.

Mummy draws two cross-looking eyes and sticks them on the glove. The children are still puzzled.

'Put the glove on, Francesca,' says Mummy. Now the girls see what it is - a five-legged spider. 'Cool!' they laugh.

# 3 March

## March

The month of March was named after Mars, the Roman god of war. March was also the marching month when the Romans usually began their battles. It is the beginning of spring and warmer weather. Flowers are blossoming, leaves are appearing on the trees, and everywhere is so much more colourful than in February.

# 4 March

If you look in the garden, you might see beautiful, bright yellow daffodils, colourful primroses and red, white, yellow or purple tulips. Up in the trees, the birds are busy building nests, laying eggs and singing sweetly. In the fields, you can see newborn baby lambs and calves with their mothers. March is a wonderful month.

 # 5 March

## Mike's Mermaid

Mike lives by the seaside, in a pretty bungalow at the end of the beach. From his bedroom window, he watches the waves splashing onto the sand and filling up the rock pools. In Summer, the beach is full of holiday makers, but in March the sands are empty and it becomes Mike's special place. Mike's mum watches him from the kitchen window as he happily explores the beach.

 # 6 March

Mike likes to scramble over to the rockpools to see what the tide has washed in. Today, he dangles his toes in the cold water and fishes for crabs and shrimps with his net. Under a clump of seaweed he can see two beady eyes and the tip of a claw. A fat, pink crab is hiding under there. Suddenly a head pops over the rocks. It's a little blonde girl, with shells and seaweed in her long, wet hair.

# 7 March

The girl is called Marina and she seems to know a lot about the creatures in the pool. Mike and Marina spend hours collecting sea creatures in Mike's bucket, until his mummy calls to tell him it's teatime. Mike wants Marina to come for tea with him, but Marina giggles and says it would be impossible. She says it's time for her to go home too.

Mike wants to play with Marina again so she tells him to send her a message.

# 8 March

When Mike asks for Marina's address, she tells him to write a note, put it in a bottle and throw into the sea! Mike thinks that would be great fun, but surely the normal post would be better! Then he sees why she wants the message in a bottle. As she waves goodbye and dives back into the sea, he sees her shiny green tail, covered in scales. 'She's a mermaid!' thinks Mike. 'I can't wait to tell my friends!' Do you think they will believe him?

## Olly to the Rescue

Olly Octopus has moved to a new home in the ocean. He is quite a shy octopus and finds it hard to make new friends. So poor Olly is feeling rather lonely.

One day, as he is swimming along the ocean floor, he hears a cry for help. Sally Swordfish is trapped under a pile of heavy boulders. Sammy Shark and Daisy Dolphin are trying to push the rocks away to free her. As soon as one rock is pushed aside, another slides down in its place.

It's a hopeless task and Olly sees that Sally is really upset. What Sammy and Daisy need is someone to hold back each rock as it is pushed to one side. They need a few extra hands, and guess what? Olly has eight! Sammy and Daisy begin clearing the rocks one by one until Olly is holding on to eight big boulders. Now Sally can escape. She shoots out of the rocks and gives Olly a big hug. Now he's a hero and everyone wants to be his friend.

# 11 March

## Mothers' Day

It will soon be Mothering Sunday and Farrah wants to make something extra special for her Mummy. She asks Granny for ideas and Granny has a good one. She takes Farrah into the garden to pick a handful of colourful flowers. Then she shows her how to arrange them on clear paper and put them inside the pages of a heavy book. Then Granny piles more heavy books on top and tells Farrah to look at them in a week or so.

# 12 March

When Farrah opens the book, she finds the flowers are still colourful, but they are also nice and flat. They have dried out beautifully and now she can arrange them on a piece of card to make a pretty picture. Granny finds an empty photo frame for her and some wrapping paper. When Mummy opens her present on Mothering Sunday, she thinks it's the best present she's ever had. Farrah spends the rest of the morning showing her Mummy and Daddy how to press flowers.

# 13 March

## Alien Invasion

James longs to be a spaceman. He has lots of books about astronauts and his bedroom walls are covered with pictures of planets and rockets. He loves make-believe games about space.

One day he runs into the garden wearing a homemade space suit, ready to tackle any fierce monsters. James doesn't know it yet, but today he's going to meet some real aliens!

# 14 March

Out in deepest, darkest space, an alien spaceship approaches our solar system.

It has been travelling for many years, looking for a new planet to live on. The creatures on the ship built the largest machine that has ever been seen on their planet. Inside, there is a huge city with plenty of room for the creatures, their animals and all their crops too. Now the captain thinks he has found a planet that looks very nice.

# 15 March

The captain lands the ship near a lake, in an area covered with tall, green plants. The aliens climb down the ladder to look around. Suddenly, the sky darkens and deafening thunder shakes the ground. Terrified aliens scramble up the ladder to safety. This planet is much too scary after all!

James is racing round the garden, fighting pretend aliens, when he senses something whizz past his nose and land next to a puddle in the long grass.

# 16 March

James kneels to take a closer look and sees a metal object, the size of an apple pip, with tiny insect-like creatures pouring out of it. As soon as his shadow falls over them, they stream back in. Then the metal pip shoots past him, way up into the sky. 'What on Earth was that?' wonders James, as he goes back to his game. Well, we know, don't we?

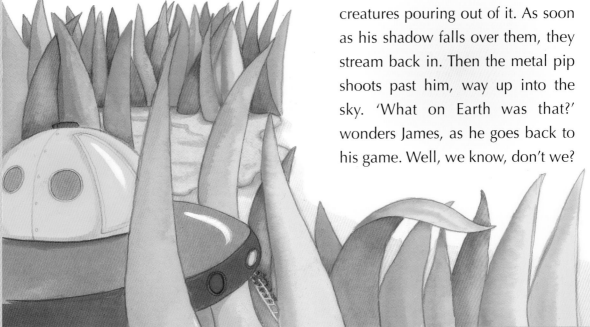

# 17 March

## Fergie's Homework

Fergie Frog has some very hard homework to do today. Maths really isn't his favourite subject, he'd much rather be playing with his brothers and sisters! Fergie can count all the way up to twenty, but when he has to add and take away numbers, it all seems much too tricky. Mummy Frog sees him struggling with his homework and thinks of a simpler way to help him do his sums.

# 18 March

Mummy calls all the family over to the pond. It's a very big family. Altogether, Fergie has nine brothers and six sisters! Mummy is going to use the children to help Fergie with his sums.

This is the first sum:

$$7 + 5 - 3 =$$

Mummy sends seven of Fergie's brothers over to a lily pad. They splash across the water, climb out and stand in line. Next she sends five of his sisters to join them.

 # 19 March

Mummy tells three of the little frogs to jump back into the pond. 'Now Fergie, count how many frogs are left on the lily pad,' she says. Fergie counts to nine. It's such an easy way to do maths homework! Fergie sends the frogs back and forth across the pond until all his sums are finished. Everyone enjoys themselves and Fergie manages to play with his family and do his homework correctly!

Tomorrow's homework will be geography. I wonder if that will be fun too!

# 20 March

## Snail Trail

It has been raining all morning, so all the slugs, snails and worms have been playing out in the downpour. They love wet weather. Now the sun is shining fiercely and they all slither back to their damp hiding places. All except Suzy Snail. Daddy Snail decides to track her down. It's quite easy because snails leave a slimy trail behind them. He soon spots her climbing up a car tyre. Not a very sensible place to be, thinks Dad. The two snails slip and slide their way back home, just in time for tea.

# 21 March

## Spring

Today is officially the first day of Spring. Outside the weather is getting warmer and the birds sing as they build nests and lay their eggs.

If you put food out for the birds, you'll see all different shapes and sizes. Here are some tips to help you recognise a few of them.

SPARROWS are small, reddish brown birds with white tummies. CROWS are big and black and very noisy!

# 22 March

Beautiful BLUE TITS have blue hats and yellow chests. Watch out for black and white MAGPIES, because they'll steal anything shiny!

JAYS are pink with blue and white wings, and blue eyes. If you're really lucky you may see a WOODPECKER, with its green feathers and red hat, pecking noisily at trees.

Perhaps you can draw some of the birds you see?

# 23 March

## Easter

Easter falls between March 22nd and April 25th each year. Christians celebrate Jesus' resurrection after the crucifixion. At Easter, it is customary to give chocolate eggs to children. There are many stories about Easter bunnies and chicks.

# 24 March

Have you ever decorated a hen's egg? Ask a grown-up to make a hole at the top and bottom of an egg and blow the yolk out. Then you can paint a face on it, but be careful not to crack it. You could draw a pirate or a clown.

Another fun game is egg rolling down a hill. The winning egg is the one that doesn't break. Don't forget to hard-boil the egg first or you'll make a big mess!

# 25 March

## Easter Egg Surprise

Bertie Bunny lives in a cosy burrow, at the bottom of a very steep hill. He's normally a very happy bunny, but today Bertie is feeling cross.

It is Easter, and at the top of the hill, a group of children are vegetable rolling. The vegetables bounce down the hill and pile up outside Bertie's door. Poor Bertie wants to go out for his lunch, but there are so many vegetables, he's completely blocked in!

# 26 March

As Bertie struggles to clear his doorway, a crowd of animals gather round to help. Once they discover that the vegetables are edible, they begin to eat their way through the pile! Bertie helps them out from his side too. Very soon the pile of vegetables has disappeared and been replaced with a pile of podgy animals! Bertie's doorway is blocked once again, but he doesn't mind anymore, because he's no longer hungry!

# 27 March

## The Wizard Grandpa

Debbie's Grandpa lives in the next street to her and he collects her from school every day. Grandpa has a secret and Debbie knows what it is, even though he hasn't told her. The secret is that her Grandpa is a wizard! Neighbours are always popping round to his flat to ask for his help, because Grandpa can repair anything.

# 28 March

When Debbie is at Grandpa's flat, she has to climb over piles of broken kettles, vacuum cleaners, radios, televisions and computers, all belonging to the neighbours. He also has a black cat, as all wizards do. Debbie discovered her Grandpa was a wizard last week. A neighbour came round to collect a cd player, which Grandpa had mended and when he got it back, he said, 'Arthur, you're a proper wizard!' So Debbie knew she was right. But 'shhhh', don't tell anyone!

# 29 March

## Danny's Dinosaurs

Danny is dinosaur mad! He has a huge collection of plastic dinosaurs and he knows all their names, even the really long ones! Danny's teacher has asked all the children in his class to bring something in that interests them, so Danny brings in his dinosaur collection. The teacher is very impressed with Danny's dinosaurs and asks him to tell his classmates a bit about them.

# 30 March

Danny tells everyone that the word dinosaur means 'thunder lizard'. These gigantic lizards lived 140 million years ago, before there were people on Earth! They came in all shapes and sizes, and they have wonderful names. He picks up the first dinosaur. 'This is a BRACHIOSAURUS, the biggest dinosaur ever. It was much, much taller than a house!' TYRANNOSAURUS REX was a very fierce dinosaur, which had teeth as long as a man's hand!

# 31 March

The PTERODACTYL was a flying dinosaur, with wings like a bat. Danny explains to the other children that the 'p' in pterodactyl is silent. Next is TRICERATOPS, with its frilly neck made from bone, and its three horns. Triceratops is Danny's favourite. The COMPSOGNATHUS was one of the smallest dinosaurs. It was about the size of a chicken. Danny's last dinosaur is a PACHYCEPHALOSAURUS.

They are also called bone-heads because they used their heads as battering rams. Afterwards, the teacher hands out paper and crayons and the children draw dinosaurs all morning. The teacher then unrolls a long piece of wallpaper and sticks the drawings all over it. Then they colour in the background with trees and volcanoes and finally they have a huge landscape, full of dinosaurs. It looks fantastic!

 **1 April**

## April Fool's Day

Paul has just moved into a new house and he is eager to make new friends. There is a little girl playing in next-door's garden, so Paul pops round to say, 'Hello'. Paul and Penny play together for half an hour until Paul's dad takes him for his first swimming lesson. There are six children in the class and Paul sees his new friend, Penny, there. This is puzzling because when he waved goodbye to her she was climbing a tree in her garden. He can't work out how she got there before him.

**2 April**

At the end of the lesson, Paul waves goodbye and tells Penny he'll see her after lunch. She nods and stifles a giggle. Ten minutes later, as Paul's dad pulls into the driveway, Paul spots Penny, still climbing trees. 'How on earth did you manage to get home before me?' asks Paul. 'I left you in the pool!' Then another car arrives and Paul sees a second Penny! 'April Fool!' the girls both shout. Then Paul realises that the girls are twins, which is great because now he has two new friends!

# 3 April

## The Grumpy Old Lady

The little old lady who lives at the bottom of our road, always looks cross. She shouts if our balls go into her garden and she shouts if we lean on her wall. She never has anything nice to say to the children round here, so we don't like her much. My mum says I don't really know her, so I can't possibly know if she's nice or not. I decide to find out. I bake a plate full of buns with my mum and I decorate each of them with icing sugar and big, fat cherries. Then I take them down to her house.

# 4 April

My knees shake as I knock at the door. The door opens and little face pokes out. 'What is it?' she asks. I take a deep breath and say, 'I've baked some buns for you, I hope you like them because I'd like to make you happy!' The old lady gives me a lovely smile and takes the buns. She's sorry for seeming grumpy, but she gets lonely sometimes. Now the nice old lady who lives at the bottom of our road is my friend. Mum says you shouldn't dislike someone if you don't know them, and she's right!

## 5 April

### Alphabet Animals

Wise Old Owl teaches in Bluebell Wood School every morning. Today, Owl wants everyone to name a different creature for every letter of the alphabet, so that they can write a poem. Each of the eight pupils has three letters. Bunny has ABC, Fox has DEF, Hen has GHI, Kingfisher has JKL, Mouse has MNO, Squirrel has PRS, Vole has TUV, Worm has WYZ and Owl has the two most difficult ones, Q and X.Everyone makes their list, then Owl helps them with the rhyme.

## 6 April

A is an ALLIGATOR
a green, scary brute,
B is a BUNNY
long-eared and cute,
C is for CAT
with lovely soft fur,
D is a DOG
who can bark but not purr,
E is for ELEPHANT
with huge trunk and ears,
F is the FOX
that Bunny here fears,
G for GIRAFFES
with long, spotty necks,
H is that HEN
who scratches and pecks,
I for IGUANA
a scaly reptile,

# 7 April

J for the JACKAL
who's often hostile,
K is for KINGFISHER
who's sitting right here,
L is a LION
whom I know you all fear,
M is for MOUSE
so dainty and sweet,
N is for NEWT
with little webbed feet,
O is for OCTOPUS
with tentacles, eight!
P is for PENGUIN
we all think they're great!
Q is a QUEEN BEE
surrounded by honey,
R is a RATTLESNAKE
scary not funny!

# 8 April

S is for SQUIRREL
a collector of nuts,
T is the TIGER
who'll be after your guts!
U is the UNICORN
made up, not true,
V is for VOLE
sitting right next to you,
W is WORM
in that hole by my tree,
X, X-RAY FISH
that live in the sea,
Y is a YAK
a peculiar sight!
And Z is for ZEBRA
with stripes, black and white.

 **9 April**

## Monster Feast

The giant troll in Monster Castle is having a cookery competition and the castle is heaving with hundreds of fairies and witches, all hoping to win the huge chest of gold, which is the first prize.

Fairies and witches don't really get on, so from that towering, black castle, you can hear voices screeching and squabbling; and pots and pans, clanging and banging; and clouds of steam, smoke and stars pouring out of the kitchen windows!

**10 April**

One by one, the cooks are eliminated, until only the two finalists remain. These are Fairy Nuf and Witch Wayupp. They bring their final three dishes to the long table in the Great Hall.

Fairy Nuf has made moonshine soup, followed by flutterby wing salad, and for pudding she has made sunlight syllabub, served in a bluebell cup. Delicious! Witch Wayupp has cooked bats' ears in filo pastry, followed by a main course of fried toads in a red wine sauce and finally, there is a magnificent tower of frogspawn profiteroles. Not so delicious!

## 11 April

Suddenly, the troll grabs Fairy Nuf and Witch Wayupp and crams them into his mouth! The witch jams her broom between his jaws and Fairy Nuf quickly casts a spell, which shrinks the troll to the size of a spider. He scuttles away into a nearby mouse-hole. The terrified witch and fairy realise that team-work has saved them from a horrible fate, and from that day onwards, all the witches and fairy folk remain good friends.

## 12 April

### Untidy Tiger

Timmy Tiger is a very untidy creature. He can never find a thing, and his den is a clutter of rubbish, books and broken toys. One day, his friends call round to see if Timmy will play football with them, but he simply cannot find his boots. Three hours later, Timmy finds the boots hidden beneath a pile of clothes, but when he reaches the field, everyone has gone home. If only Timmy's den had not been such a mess! From now on, he's going to be a very tidy tiger!

# 13 April

## Our Planets

If you look up into the sky on a clear night, you will see hundreds of twinkling stars. Each tiny star is really a huge ball of fire, billions of miles away. But there is one star, which is much closer to our planet. Can you guess which it is? Yes, it's our very own sun. Our sun keeps us warm and gives us light. There are nine planets in our solar system, but Earth is the only planet which has creatures living on it.

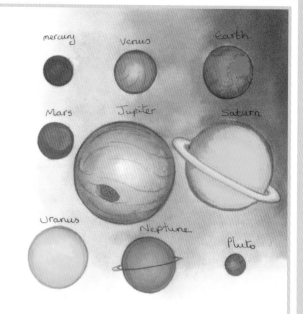

# 14 April

MERCURY: Is the nearest to the sun. VENUS: Can sometimes be seen in the morning. EARTH: This is our planet. MARS: The red planet. JUPITER: Is the largest. SATURN: A beautiful, ringed, yellow planet. URANUS: Has a summer which lasts for forty years. Imagine that! NEPTUNE: Is a large blue planet. PLUTO: Is the farthest from the sun.

# 15 April

It can be difficult to remember the order of the planets, but one way is to think of a sentence using the first letter of each planet. Try this:

My Vole Eats Mummy's Jam Sandwich Under Nicky's Piano. Why don't you try making one up yourself?

# 16 April

## Silly Dilly

Dilly Duck is the vainest duck you ever met! She spends all day paddling up and down the river, gazing at her reflection, and not looking where she is going. One bright, sunny morning, while she glides upriver, smiling at herself, she tips over the edge of the weir and into the filthy, churning water below. It takes her ages to scramble back up the weir, and when she does, everyone falls about laughing, because she is such a mess! Next time maybe she'll be less vain and watch where she's going!

# 17 April

## The Sad Little Starfish

Little Starfish lives in the ocean with lots of other sea creatures. He is surrounded by crabs, fish, shrimp, sharks and jellyfish, but he'd really like to meet someone just like him. Each night he searches the sea-bed, but he can never seem to find another starfish. One night, the waves are stronger than usual and little starfish is washed up onto a beach.

# 18 April

He crawls towards an outcrop of rocks, hoping to find a quiet rock pool, in which to spend the night. By the time he reaches the rocks, he's exhausted and lies quietly on a stone, gazing up at the sky. It is awash with twinkling stars, which look a bit like him! Whilst he is smiling up at the stars, he hears something splashing out of the rock pool. It's another little starfish! She also watches the stars at night, as she's lonely too. Now the two have met, they are sure to live happily ever after.

## 19 April

### The Rowdy Recorder

Millie is learning to play the recorder at school. She practises at home every day, but unfortunately she's not very musical and her family are always complaining about the dreadful noise. Millie doesn't care, she carries her recorder with her everywhere she goes so that she can practise. Today the family are going to the seaside. The children explore the rock pools while Mummy and Daddy lay out the picnic. Later, as the sun sinks low in the sky, the parents decide it's time to leave.

## 20 April

Mummy calls the children over, but there is no sign of either of them. Out amongst the rock pools, the tide has turned and the children are trapped on the rocks. They call for help, but the crashing of the waves drowns their voices. Millie's sister begins to cry and Millie thinks of a way to guide her parents to them. She blows as hard as she can on the recorder. Within minutes, they have been found. What a good job Millie had her recorder with her. No one will ever complain about it again!

 # 21 April

## A Change For Caterpillar

Each morning Snake and Frog follow the same pathway to the river. One morning, as they pass the big, old tree where Caterpillar lives, Snake notices something strange hanging from a low branch.

'What do you think that is?' he asks. 'Well it looks like a leaf, but it doesn't match the other leaves,' says Frog. 'Perhaps Caterpillar knows.' But little Caterpillar is nowhere to be found!

# 22 April

A few days later, as Frog and Snake pass the tree, they show Toucan and Lion the strange object. Toucan doesn't know what it is either, but Lion recognises it to be a chrysalis. He says, 'If you look closely you can see lots more of them hidden in the tree.' Then, as they crowd around the tree, the chrysalis suddenly begins to wriggle. 'It's alive!' Toucan screeches in alarm. Lion laughs and says, 'I'll let Caterpillar explain it to you tomorrow!'

# 23 April

The next day, they gather round the tree and the chrysalis wriggles and shakes until its little sack splits. Out crawls a beautiful butterfly. She flutters around the animals' heads. 'Hi guys, I'm back!' she squeaks. Snake is puzzled. 'I know that voice but you're not Caterpillar!'

Butterfly smiles, 'Half our lives, we're caterpillars and for the rest we're butterflies. But it's still me.' Around them, hundreds of butterflies emerge. Toucan laughs, 'It's all very confusing, but now I can race you to the river!' And they fly off, with their friends racing after them.

# 24 April

## Black Sheep Of The Family

Shona sheep is painting a picture for Sheila's birthday. First she splashes on a line of green grass, then a bright blue sky and then a colourful scarecrow. It looks great, but Shona thinks it needs something else to finish it off. She adds a black crow. Then, as she steps back to admire the picture, she knocks the paint over, colouring everything black! When Sheila arrives she asks what the painting is. 'Er, it's a black sheep, in a field at night!' mumbles Shona. Amazingly, Sheila loves her present, because it's so unusual. Clever Shona!

## 25 April

### Back To Bed

Maisie Mouse doesn't want to go to church today, so she has used a felt tipped pen to draw red spots all over her face. Mummy is horrified when she sees her and says, kindly, 'Back to bed, you're ill.' Mummy tucks Maisie up with hot soup and some comics. Maisie feels rather clever. After an hour or two she creeps downstairs to go outside in the sunshine. 'Back to bed, you're ill,' shouts Granny. She has seen a lot of smudgy, red marks on the pillow and suspects mischief.

## 26 April

Maisie is very bored now. She has read all her comics and she can hear her brother watching television downstairs. She makes another attempt to leave her bed, but as soon as she moves, she hears Granny's voice bellowing up the stairs, 'Back up to bed, you're ill.' Millie is really fed up now. She decides to escape and climbs out of her bedroom window, before running off to have a cool dip in the river.

## 27 April

Maisie is splashing around in the water when she sees Granny and Mummy thundering down the path. 'Back to bed, you're ill,' they both shout. 'But I'm feeling better now,' says Maisie. She wonders why Mummy looks so cross. Then she notices long red streaks of felt tip, smudging down her fur. Mummy says, 'You obviously have an illness known as *Reddus stripus pretendus*, so… Back to bed, you're ill!' Silly Maisie. I don't think she'll try that again!

## 28 April

### The Greedy Pirate

Captain Rich Pickens is a very greedy pirate. He captures ships and sails away with all their gold and jewels. But his pirate ship isn't very big and soon the hold, the deck and all the rooms fill up with treasure. The crew worry that their ship may sink and ask the captain if they can go home, but greedy Captain Pickens doesn't know when to stop. Then, one breezy April afternoon, the lookout spies a galleon on the horizon. The pirates race after the ship and capture it.

## 29 April

The ship is full of precious jewels and coins, but the captured captain warns the pirates that their ship will not be able to stand the extra weight. The crew agree with their prisoner, but Captain Pickens will not listen and orders his men to haul a giant treasure chest onboard. The ship begins to groan under its burden. Then, quietly at first, there is the sound of splintering wood and nails popping. The crew realise the ship is breaking up and throw the chest back, but it's no use so they rapidly abandon ship.

## 30 April

All except for Captain Pickens, who refuses to leave and who is soon ankle deep in water! The captain of the other ship is back in charge and offers to help the crew if they give up piracy and work for him. The crew are happy to agree, but Captain Pickens refuses and is sent off in a little rowing boat. He'll probably spend the rest of his days rowing around the site of his sunken ship, trying to work out a way to salvage his treasure. Some people never learn!

# 1 May

## The Lost Wellies

James lives on a farm. It's often quite muddy so there are always lots of Wellington boots to be found - and lost. James always seems to lose his left boot. Today he discovers that, yet again, a left boot is missing. Dad is cross and refuses to buy another new pair, so James must borrow one of Dad's spares, (which are too enormous to walk in!), or borrow one of Mum's, (which are pink!), or he can search again to find the lost welly. He chooses the last option!

James looks everywhere, until only the duck pond is left. As he searches through the reeds, James sees his blue boot hidden near the water's edge. Bending down to retrieve it, he finds a nest of eggs inside the boot! James doesn't know what to do, as he can't disturb the nest. Then he spots something bobbing up and down near the lily pads. It's the red boot he lost last month. Hurray! Now he can wear the old red boot with the blue boot he has at home!

 ## 2 May

### Hilda's Hen House

Hilda Hen wants to decorate the hen house, so she asks all the other hens which colour they like the best. Helen Hen likes daffodil yellow, Heather Hen prefers a lovely sky blue, Holly Hen prefers holly berry red, but Hilda Hen's favourite colour is pink. Hilda doesn't know which colour to pick, because she doesn't want to upset any of her friends. In the end, she paints the walls yellow, the roof red, the door blue and the window frame pink. Everyone is happy!

 ## 3 May

### Daydreaming Darren

Darren is a daydreamer. Instead of paying attention at school he imagines being a fighter pilot. Or a famous lawyer, a pop star or maybe a television personality. Anything but pay attention to his school lessons. One day, a famous television sports presenter visits Darren's school to talk about careers. The guest asks the children if any of them have thought about a career as a sports presenter.

# 4 May

Darren's hand shoots up. The man asks him if there is a particular sport that he is good at. Darren shakes his head. He spends too much of his time daydreaming to practise much sport. The man asks if Darren is good at English or Drama. But again Darren shakes his head. He is far too busy daydreaming to do his English homework. Or his Maths, Science, Geography, or anything really.

# 5 May

The presenter says that if the children want to have an interesting career, the most important step is to work hard and pay attention at school.

Darren thinks maybe he should listen to his teacher in future, because he really would like to be successful, like the guest. He is suddenly aware that it is very quiet in the classroom and looks up to see that lesson time is over and everyone has left. Oops, Darren has been daydreaming again!

 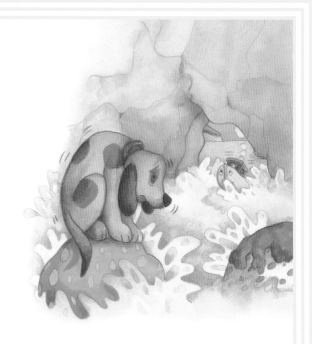

# 6 May

## Timmy the Tug Boat

Timmy is a little tugboat with big ideas. He wants to be a lifeboat and rescue people in danger. But the bigger lifeboats laugh at Timmy and tell him he is far too small to be any help. They look so important and busy that Timmy tries to keep out of their way. He spends most days just chugging up and down the coast, keeping a look out for anyone in distress.

# 7 May

One day, as Timmy is passing the cliffs near the beach, he hears frantic barking, which seems to be coming from one of the caves. Timmy knows that the caves are fun to explore at low tide, but as high tide approaches, the caves begin to fill with water. Timmy thinks the dog must have gone inside earlier and is now trapped. Timmy rings his bell to alert the lifeboats, and waits outside.

# 8 May

Two big, strong lifeboats arrive within minutes. 'Stand back, Timmy. You can leave this to us,' they call. The boats take turns to try and squeeze through the narrow cave opening, but they are far too wide. The dog sounds really frightened now and Timmy worries the rising sea might sweep it away.

Timmy decides he must help and launches himself through the opening. He reaches the stranded dog, seconds before a big wave sweeps into the cave, covering the rock it had been clinging to. When Timmy emerges from the cave with the grateful dog, it's to a hero's welcome from the big lifeboats. From now on, brave little Timmy will patrol alongside the big boats, because who knows when they may need him next!

# 9 May

## Another Boring Birthday

Today it is Tracy's fifth birthday and she can't be bothered to open any of her presents. She already has everything that she has ever asked for: the biggest doll, the most expensive clothes, the best toys in the toy store and all the board games you could want. Her parents tell her she's lucky and are cross when she's not grateful, but birthdays are not too exciting when you are spoiled. This year, when asked what she would like, she said 'Nothing,' because she just couldn't be bothered to think. There is only one parcel this year, which is unusual.

# 10 May

It's in a very big box, even bigger than Tracy, and it's strangely light! Finally, there is a glimmer of interest. Tracy peels away the wrapping paper to reveal a big box of...NOTHING! 'Which is exactly what you asked for,' says Daddy, and he leaves her with her present. Tracy is so cross that she decides to ignore her family and stay in the box all day! After a while she gets bored and pokes a hole in the side with her finger. It looks a bit like a window. Then she tears a flap off at one side, which looks a bit like a door.

 # 11 May

With a little more effort, the box begins to resemble a house. Tracy scribbles over the box, drawing bricks and flowers, then she sticky tapes bits of material to the windows to make curtains. She begins to enjoy herself. Tracy grabs a cushion from her bed and a couple of dolls and has a little tea party in her play-house. In no time at all it's lunchtime and Tracy asks if her friends can come over to play in her play-house. She hasn't been bored at all. In fact, she thinks this is the best birthday ever. All she needed was a little imagination.

# 12 May

## A Very Special Dog

Lenny is a Labrador puppy with a very special job. He is a seeing dog. Lenny belongs to a young lady called Pippa, who is blind. Lenny has been trained to help guide Pippa safely wherever she goes. He knows he must never chase cats or play with other dogs when he is working, but he really doesn't mind because he gets to do all sorts of exciting things, like riding trains and buses, and guiding Pippa around the shops and streets. Lenny thinks he is the luckiest dog in the world.

# 13 May

## Computer Quarrels

Gillian, Jeremy and Dinah seem to spend most of their school holidays arguing over who will play whom on the computer. They squabble over the chairs, the controls, who's winning, who's losing and Mummy has just had enough! She removes the computer, unplugs the television and hides away all the electronic games. Silence at last! After a while, Mummy creeps downstairs to see what the three children are up to.

# 14 May

The children have dug out a pile of old board games from the cupboard under the stairs, and are engrossed in a game. A little while later, they disappear into the garden to play French cricket with an old tennis racquet. When friends pop round in the afternoon with a new computer game, they end up joining in with the outdoor games. Gillian, Jeremy and Dinah have been such good children that Mummy says they can have their computer and television back. 'No thanks,' they all shout. 'It's more fun without them!'

# 15 May

## Digging Dennis

Dennis the Dog loves digging holes for his bones. He digs holes all over old Mrs Mottram's garden. Mrs Mottram sighs when she sees her ruined flowerbeds. It will take her all day to replant the flowers and she still has the vegetable patch to dig over. Her old bones are aching before she even picks up the spade! Then she has an idea. She gathers up the flowers in a basket and, putting on her hat and coat, she heads off to the florist shop.

The florist is happy to buy Mrs Mottram's flowers. She can make beautiful flower arrangements to sell in her shop. With the money she gets, Mrs Mottram buys some sausages for tea and a dozen large marrow bones. She goes home and tosses the bones into the vegetable patch. Dennis is happy to bury the bones, which helpfully digs over the soil. Now it's easy to plant the seeds! It's soon teatime and Mrs Mottram has a big plate of sausage and mash. I think she's earned it, don't you?

# 16 May

## Wally Warthog's Wish

Wally Warthog lives in the forest. He is covered in bristly, black hair and has a lumpy, bumpy sort of skin. He has a pair of long, sharp tusks either side of a podgy, little snout. Wally wishes he was handsome and worries that the other forest animals are laughing at him because he's so ugly. He tries to keep away from everyone and that makes him a very lonely warthog.

# 17 May

Wally sees Freddy Fox and wishes he had beautiful, red fur like him. He sees Sally Squirrel and wishes he had a fantastic, bushy tail like her. He sees Milly and Molly Mouse and wishes he had a dainty little nose like them. Then he sees someone new to the forest, although there is something strangely familiar about her. She has the same shuffling walk as Wally. The same gleaming white tusks, strong bristly hair and cute little tail!

## 18 May

She is ambling along, pushing her snout through the leaves and looking for something tasty to eat, when she spots him. She smiles at Wally and blushes prettily. Her name is Winnie Warthog and she thinks Wally is the most handsome creature she has ever seen! Wally thinks Winnie is beautiful too. For the first time in their lives, the two warthogs feel happy with the way they look. They decide they are made for each other and live happily ever after.

## 19 May

### The Mysterious Animal

Jane and Helen are playing in their garden, when Helen sees something moving under the hedge. The girls reach in and pull out an extraordinary looking creature. What could it be? It has a duck-like beak and webbed feet, but it can't be a duck because it has fur, not feathers! Jane thinks it might be an otter, but otters don't have paddle-shaped tails. The girls seach for more clues under the hedge and soon find a nest with two small eggs inside.

# 20 May

The girls decide to ask Daddy if he knows what it is. Daddy is also puzzled and thinks the girls are playing a joke on him, until he looks under the hedge. Helen says it must be a bird, because it lays eggs. Jane insists it's an animal, because of its four legs. Daddy decides to ring the local zoo. The Zookeeper asks Daddy to put the creature in a cardboard box and bring it to the zoo. He thinks he knows what it is!

# 21 May

The animal escaped from the Zoo last week and he is really pleased to have her back. He explains that she is an Australian duck-billed platypus. He tells the girls that these are one of the few mammals that lay eggs, and these eggs should be hatching any time now! A few days later, when Helen and Jane visit the Zoo, the Zookeeper shows them two newborn, baby platypuses. They are really cute, and guess what they are called? Jane and Helen!

## 22 May

### Gertie Ghost

Gertie ghost lives all alone in a ramshackle old house in the country. All the windows are broken or boarded up and most of the doors are swinging on broken hinges. No one would want to live in such a run down house unless, of course, they were a ghost! One day a team of builders and decorators move into the house. Gertie's peace is shattered by lots of hammering, drilling and sawing.

## 23 May

Gertie is very cross and tries to scare the men away. She moans loudly as she floats through floors and ceilings, slamming doors around her. The workmen are so scared that they work twice as fast so they can finish and leave! Word gets around about the haunted house and soon there are coach loads of tourists, trailing around, taking photos. It's all too much for Gertie and she packs her bags and goes in search of another ramshackle old house. So, now you know how to get rid of ghosts!

 **24** **May**

## The Jungle Hospital

Leo Lion is in hospital with a broken leg. He feels very sorry for himself. Nurse Elephant has put his injured leg in plaster and tucked him up in bed. Leo looks around at the other patients. In the next bed is Sally Snake with a sore throat. She is swaddled in thick, woolly scarves to keep her throat warm. Then there is Timmy Tiger who is covered in itchy, red spots and can't stop scratching!

**25** **May**

Opposite Leo is Fenella Flamingo who has eaten something strange and has turned a bit green! No one is talking because they are all too busy feeling sorry for themselves. Suddenly the ward doors are flung open and Philip Frog trundles into the room in a wheelchair. Philip lost both his legs in an accident some time ago, but he is still as full of fun as ever. Nurse Elephant has asked Philip to come in to cheer everyone up.

## 26 May

Philip spins around the room, talking to everyone and making them smile. Soon the room is buzzing with chatter and laughter. Philip stays for an hour and when he leaves, he promises to return the next day. Everyone feels so much better after his visit. Nurse Elephant tells her patients that it is no use feeling sorry for themselves because there's always someone worse off than they are. The animals nod and smile and chat away for the rest of the day. And they can't wait to see Philip tomorrow!

## 27 May

### Diana's Daisy Chain

Diana is always picking wild flowers for her Mummy. There are vases of wild flowers all over the house, making it look very pretty. Diana likes to look pretty too, so she runs into the garden to gather some daisies. With her fingernails, she makes a small slit in each daisy stem, then threads the stems through each hole. Soon she has a really long daisy chain, which she winds around her arms and shoulders. Clever Diana, doesn't she look pretty?

## 28 May

### Donny Digger

Little Donny Digger lives on a building site, where a new supermarket is being built. Every day, Donny watches the big diggers preparing the ground. They scrape out great piles of earth and lumber back and forth across the building site, looking very important. Donny longs to join in but the big diggers tell him he's far too small and he'll just get in the way. Poor Donny!

## 29 May

Each of the diggers has a big strong driver, but one day a new driver arrives who is much shorter than the others. It's difficult to find the right machine for Tommy, as most diggers are too big for him. When Tommy sees little Donny, he realises they are perfect for each other. Donny and Tommy are good at doing all the fiddly little jobs that are hard for bigger diggers, and that makes them very happy.

## 30 May

### Molly's Teeth

Today, Molly is going to the dentist for a check-up. She feels a little nervous because she doesn't want to have a filling. When she arrives at the dentist's surgery, she sees her friend Sarah climbing into the dentist's chair. Sarah's mummy says Sarah has eaten too many sweets and needs a filling. Poor Sarah! First Sarah has an injection in her mouth, which isn't too bad. Then the dentist repairs her tooth and tells her not to eat so many sweets.

## 31 May

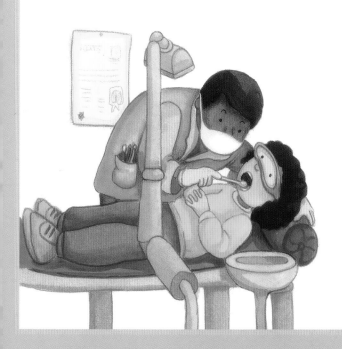

Soon it's Molly's turn. She sits in the big chair and opens her mouth wide. The dentist has a light and a small round mirror to check her teeth. He is smiling because Molly's teeth are healthy and don't need treating. He knows Molly must clean her teeth regularly and that she must eat lots of fresh fruit and vegetables, instead of sweets. Mummy is very proud of Molly and lets her have a treat from the shops. Molly chooses a juicy red apple!

 # 1 June

## Charlie The Clown

All Charlie's family have been clowns for as long as anyone can remember and it is expected that Charlie will be a clown too. The trouble is, Charlie would rather be a high wire, or trapeze artiste, but no one will listen to him. Whenever he can find the time, he practises balancing and walking across his Mum's washing line.

# 2 June

One day, Charlie sees a little old lady chasing a kitten past his caravan. The kitten runs into the Big Top and scrambles high up the main pole. Charlie peers into the tent and asks if he can help. The kitten won't move and the old lady is crying. To reach the kitten, Charlie must climb a ladder, cross a high wire and use the trapeze to reach the main pole.

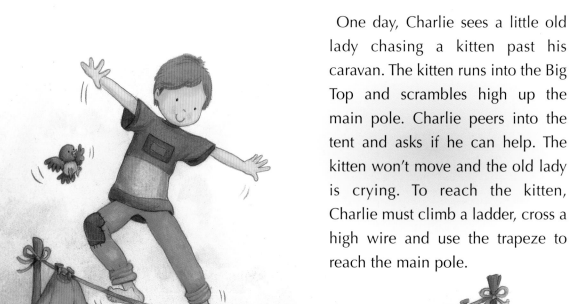

# 3 June

Charlie's parents arrive just as he's about to cross the high wire. They shout at him to turn back, but Charlie is concentrating too hard to hear them. He's nearly there now. Just half a metre to go, and yes, he makes it across the wire safely! Then he reaches for the trapeze and with a huge jump he launches himself high into the air. Everyone holds their breath as Charlie somersaults and lands neatly next to the kitten.

# 4 June

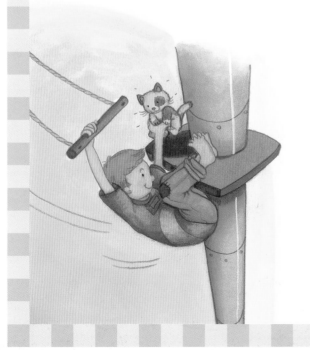

Charlie scoops the kitten into his arms and jumps off the platform into the safety net. Everybody cheers. The little old lady says Charlie is a hero and can't thank him enough. Mum and Dad are so impressed with Charlie's skills that they tell him he can start training for the high wire if that's what he wants. Charlie can't wait!

 **5** June

### Jungle Sports Day

Today is Sports Day in the jungle and the first event is the three-legged race. The animals stand at the starting line. Giraffe, Rhino and Elephant are strapped together. Lion, Zebra and Crocodile are also tied together. In the third group are Tortoise, Sloth and Turtle. The bigger animals snigger when they see this little trio, they don't think there will be any competition from them!

 **6** June

Hippo raises the starting flag. 'Ready, steady, GO!'

As they whiz past the coconut palms, Elephant's group are just in front. They round a corner and head towards a tangle of jungle vines. 'Duck!' cries Rhino. But it's too late. Giraffe's neck becomes entangled in the vines and they grind to a halt.

Lion, Zebra and Crocodile surge ahead, but they don't see the huge, sticky spider's web, which stretches across the track.

Far behind everyone else, the last little trio plod on. They are surprised when they overtake Elephant's group, frantically trying to pull Giraffe free. They are even more surprised when they pass Lion's group, all caught up in a giant, sticky web. But they simply can't believe it when they hobble past the finishing post in first place! Turtle, Sloth and Tortoise are the winners and they get the trophy. Well done to the slow coaches!

# 8 June

## A Miniature Zoo

Maddie is having a bug hunt in her garden. She is listing all the different types of insects and sketching them. Under rocks she finds earwigs, spiders, woodlice and centipedes. In the trees are tiny red spiders, bright green caterpillars and lots of flies.

Around the flowers are Maddie's favourite creatures, stripy bees, colourful butterflies and spotty red ladybirds. When she grows up, Maddie would like to be an entomologist and study insects everyday.

# 9 June

## The Flower Garden

Last month, Carlie and her Dad bought a dozen trays of bedding plants for their garden. Carlie didn't think they were very interesting, in fact they looked rather like bunches of weeds! Dad showed Carlie how to plant the seedlings without damaging their roots, then they sprinkled pellets around to keep the greedy snails away, watered them and then waited.

marigold

Petunia

aubrietia

geranium

lobelia

# 10 June

Over the following weeks, Carlie forgot all about the plants, but today she is going to see if they have grown. As Carlie walks into the garden, she gasps at the rainbow of colours she sees. All the plants have blossomed and Dad teaches Carlie their names. Blue lobelia, purple aubrieta, red geraniums, bright, yellow marigolds and petunias in every colour imaginable. Do you have any of these plants in your garden?

# 11 June

## Fat Cat

Tommy's cat is getting fat. She seems to get rounder everyday! Tommy tells his mum that he's worried Fliss might burst if she keeps on growing. Mummy tells Tommy not to worry because Fliss isn't being greedy. She has lots of babies growing in her tummy and they could be born at any time. When Tommy gently strokes Fliss' tummy, he can feel the babies moving inside.

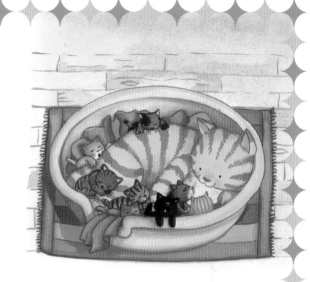

# 12 June

One day, when Tommy gets back from school, his mummy calls him into the kitchen. He sees Fliss surrounded by eight mewing bundles of fur. All the kittens have their eyes closed. When the kittens are old enough to leave Fliss, they will all go to good homes, but Tommy pleads to be able to keep one. Mummy agrees and Tommy chooses a little black kitten with a white mark on her nose. He decides to call her Floss. Isn't Tommy lucky!

# 13 June

## Fathers' Day

Daddy is fast asleep in bed when a noise awakens him. It's the rattle of a cup, saucer and plate on a tray! Standing by the bed are Joe and Mummy with tea, toast and a big envelope. 'Happy Fathers' Day!' shouts Joe. Joe can't afford a present, so he's going to help Daddy all day. They walk the dog, weed the garden and wash the car together. Daddy says it's been the best Fathers' Day ever!

# 14 June

## Silly Sammy

Sammy is always in trouble. Everyone tells her she's messy and clumsy, which makes her feel useless and sad. Today, Sammy's cousin is here and Mummy has put the toddler in a playpen. Sammy blocks her ears as the toddler is screaming so loudly. Mummy tells Sammy to keep the little boy amused while she hangs out the washing, but Sammy hasn't a clue what to do.

# 15 June

Sammy wonders if the toddler might be thirsty after making so much noise, so she runs off to get a beaker of water. As she comes back into the room, Sammy trips over one of her toys and falls flat on her face in front of the playpen, spilling water all over the carpet. The toddler stops howling and watches with interest. Sammy is horrified!

# 16 June

The puddle of water sinks into the carpet, so Sammy tries to grab the tissue box and accidentally knocks a pile of washing over her head! Then she hears Mummy coming back and, looking at the awful mess around her, knows she's going to get into trouble. But as Mummy comes through the door, the toddler is laughing and clapping his hands. Mummy gives Sammy a big hug for cheering the little boy up. I don't think Sammy feels useless anymore, do you?

# 17 June

## School Sports

One sunny, Saturday morning, Johnny Rabbit leaps out of bed, pulls on his school tracksuit and heads for the school playing fields with his kit in one hand and a piece of jam and toast in the other. The football team are looking for new players and Johnny is desperate to be picked. When he reaches the field he sees that it is shared by the cricket team, who are also looking for new players.

# 18 June

The football coach blows his whistle and the teams kick off. Johnny sees there are a lot of good players here and worries that he may not be good enough. The coach finally blows his whistle and the players gather round to hear who's been selected. Johnny is really disappointed when his name is not read out. He wonders if the cricket team need more players, but they're packing up too.

# 19 June

As he stands at the edge of the pitch, he hears a frightened mew from the tree above his head. Two big, fat crows are bullying a tiny kitten. Johnny grabs handfuls of mud to throw at the crows. He hits them squarely on their tails and they fly away squawking noisily. The frightened kitten is now wobbling dangerously and suddenly she topples off the branch.

# 20 June

Johnny leaps forwards and catches the kitten before she hits the ground. The cricket coach has been watching Johnny and is very impressed with his quick thinking, accurate shots and clever catching. He asks Johnny if he would like to join the cricket team. Johnny is thrilled and agrees to join. He can't wait to get home and tell his mum and dad.

# 21 June

## Midsummer's Day

Today is the summer solstice, when the earth is closest to the sun. This means that we have the shortest night and the longest day of the year in the UK. After today, the days will gradually become shorter until, in six months' time, we will have the shortest day and the longest night, on the 21st December.

# 22 June

## The Unhaunted House

Rosie Rat is a timid little creature and all her school friends tease her, so she has thought of a plan to make them think she's brave. At the end of an overgrown lane, by the wood, stands a tumbledown old house that everyone thinks is haunted. Rosie's school friends are daring each other to spend a night in the old house. No one is brave enough, except Rosie!

## 23 June

The other animals can hardly believe that timid little Rosie will go through with it. They walk with her to the house that night and wave goodbye. The heavy front door creaks open and Rosie disappears inside. As she walks through the rooms, the floorboards squeak and groan. Outside, the school friends are so scared by the spooky noises that they all run home to bed!

## 24 June

Rosie climbs the rotting staircase and tiptoes into the main bedroom. As she climbs onto the old bed, she can hear slow footsteps coming up the stairs behind her. Then the bedroom door creaks open. 'Hello, Aunty Ruth and Uncle Ross,' says Rosie. 'Can I stay for the night?' Rosie's aunt and uncle live here, in this quiet, old house. Rosie can't wait to see her friends in the morning. She knows they'll never tease her about being timid again!

# 25 June

## Wizards and Witches

Stories of Wilfrid the Wizard and Winifrid Witch, and their golden tree, have stopped many brave men from venturing into the Wild Wood in search of treasure. None who have entered the wood have ever returned, and so the legend lives on. Anthony lives in a village just outside the Wild Wood. He plans to find his way to the Wizard and Witch's cottage and bring back a branch of the golden tree.

# 26 June

Anthony hopes the branch will bring him fame and fortune, so he will be able to ask Miranda to marry him. One sunny day in June, Anthony rides into the wood. He is gone for many weeks and Miranda worries that she may never see him again. When he finally emerges from the wood, he is tired and miserable but everyone wants to hear his story. Anthony tells them that he searched the woods for weeks before coming across a derelict cottage.

## 27 June

The building had not been used for centuries. He knew that the Witch and Wizard had once lived there, because inside he found old spell books, mysterious looking jars and a broken cauldron. In the garden, Anthony uncovered a cracked headstone where Wilfrid and Winifrid had been buried, hundreds of years ago. Next to it stood a tree covered in golden blossom, but there was nothing special about this tree, it was just an ordinary yellow laburnum.

## 28 June

Filled with disappointment, Anthony found his way back home. He didn't think Miranda would want to marry a penniless youth, but he was wrong. Miranda thought Anthony was the bravest person she had ever met and wanted to marry him and live in the derelict cottage. Since it was now safe to enter the wood, they could make a living hunting there. So Anthony and Miranda lived happily ever after.

# 29 June

## Summer Holiday

The Mouse family are off on their summer holiday today. Dad has bought a second hand caravan and the family are filling it with clothes, toys and lots of cheese! Soon they are off in their little, red car. It's nearly lunchtime when they arrive at the coast. Milly and Molly have never seen the sea before and they can't wait to have a paddle. They grab cheese sandwiches and race down onto the beach.

# 30 June

The whole family spend ages leaping over waves and splashing about in the water. Then they get dry and start building giant sandcastles. Dad's is the biggest! Soon, it's time for bed and the girls are really excited to be sleeping in the cosy caravan. Mummy is not sure they will get any sleep at all. Outside the caravan, the seagulls are squawking and the waves crash noisily onto the beach, but nothing can keep these two little girls awake a moment longer – all that fresh air has worn them out!

# 1 July

## Sandy's Washing Machine

Sandy's Mum is always busy, so Sandy decides to give her a helping hand. She often watches Mum doing the washing and she's sure she can manage it all by herself. Sandy loads the washing machine with Mum's best woolly cardigan, Sandy's white tee shirt, two white towels and Dad's red socks. She adds the powder and turns the machine to boil wash.

# 2 July

An hour later, Sandy has a big surprise! Something magical has happened. The washing has been mysteriously replaced with different clothes! She shows the clothes to her Mum, who is as surprised as Sandy. There's a tiny, doll-sized cardigan, a pink tee shirt, two pink towels and, to Sandy's surprise, her Dad's red socks.

Mum says Sandy has been very helpful but she'd like to do the washing herself next time!

# 3 July

## Tough Tommy

Tommy is a big, blue truck. He's very strong and can carry almost anything. Last week he drove two enormous elephants from one zoo to another, fifty miles away. It's all in a days work for Tommy the Truck.

Tommy likes the way that everyone looks up to him, but he has a secret fear. Tommy worries that one day he may have to use his horn.

# 4 July

Tommy would love a great, booming horn, but his just makes an embarrassing squeak! Tommy can't bear the thought of everyone laughing at him.

To avoid using his horn, Tommy will not drive anywhere that is busy. He drives through the quiet countryside where he's unlikely to meet anyone, but this makes his journeys much longer than they need to be.

 # 5 July

Today is July 5th and Tommy is exactly one year old. There is to be a big birthday party this afternoon with all the other trucks from Tommy's yard. But there is one little problem. Tommy still has one last delivery to make and if he goes the long way round, he will be late for his own party. Poor Tommy. Whatever can he do?

 # 6 July

The other trucks don't know why Tommy is sad, but to cheer him up they give him their present before he leaves. He rips off the paper and can't believe his luck when he opens the box. It's a big, shiny, fabulously noisy horn! Tommy is delighted. Now he can go the shorter routes and use his horn as much as he needs. He races off with the final load and is soon back in time to enjoy his party

 **7 July**

## Sammy Centipede

It is the day before the new school term and the jungle animals are getting their uniforms ready. The school shop has stocked up on caps, blazers, shirts and shoes - especially shoes! The queue outside the shop reaches back a long, long way because Sammy Centipede is at the front of the queue trying on new shoes. He'll need fifty pairs of shoes! Everyone wishes they had got to the shop before Sammy. I hope there will be some shoes left for everyone else!

 **8 July**

## Ted the Decorator

Ted is watching Daddy decorating the hall. First, Daddy measures the wall and the wallpaper. Then he cuts the right lengths of paper, coats them with paste and hangs them onto the wall. He smoothes out all the little bumps and bubbles with a brush and stands back to admire his handiwork. Ted thinks the hall looks really nice with bright yellow wallpaper, much nicer than his boring blue bedroom.

Daddy clears away all the sticky bits of paper and stacks the decorating table and paste bucket against the wall in the garage. His next job is to mow the lawn before lunch. Ted thinks it looks quite easy to hang wallpaper and there are quite a lot of spare rolls left over. He thinks it would be a shame to waste them! Daddy is mowing in the garden, Mummy is cooking in the kitchen and Ted is decorating in his bedroom!

## 10 July

Ted cuts, pastes, hangs and smoothes. Two hours later he finishes the room and looks for the doorway, but it's nowhere to be seen. He looks for the window, but that's disappeared too! He decides to shout. 'HELP!!!' Mummy and Daddy burst through the papered doorway to find a proud but sticky bear in his newly decorated bedroom. They can't be cross because Ted was only trying to help, but Daddy thinks Ted might need a helping hand next time!

# 11 July

## The Joke's On Annie

Annie is always playing annoying tricks on her family and they sometimes get a little tired of her odd sense of humour.

Today, the family are having a day in the country and Mummy has packed a picnic for everyone. They arrive at a park, full of massive boulders, which are perfect for scrambling up.

# 12 July

Jonathan and Annie climb a big rock and when Annie reaches the top she leans over the side to see a long, long drop. Just below the edge is a wide ledge. Annie thinks up another trick. She hangs over the top of the rock and shouts at her brother to help and then ducks out of sight on the ledge below. Jonathan is horrified and rushes to the top of the boulder, just as Annie pops up with a big grin on her face.

## 13 July

Jonathan is really fed up of his little sister's silly pranks. Mummy and Daddy have laid out a picnic at the bottom of the rock, so the children climb back down for lunch. After lunch, the children tidy the picnic away and pack everything in the car. Mummy and Daddy stroll down to the riverbank to have a quiet read by the water's edge. Jonathan grabs his book and runs down to join them.

## 14 July

Annie roots around in the car for her book and accidentally locks herself in! She calls out to the rest of the family to unlock the car, but Dad just shakes his head and tells her to stop pretending. Everyone is bored of Annie's constant tricks. Poor Annie spends the next hour locked in the car, because everyone thinks she is joking. Annie doesn't think she wants to play tricks anymore.

 # 15 July

## Keep Off The Drive!

Daddy is cementing the driveway. He has borrowed a mixer from the building site he works at and has made huge piles of cement. Short lengths of wood at the edge of the drive stop the cement from leaking onto the garden and Daddy carefully spreads the cement evenly down the drive. It takes a few hours to set, so Daddy and Nicola make lots of 'KEEP OFF' notices and stick them all around the drive.

# 16 July

Daddy and Nicola are visiting Grandma this afternoon and they expect the cement to be set by the time they return. Daddy is very proud of his new drive, but Nicola thinks it looks a bit boring. She prefers the old, cracked flagstones with sprouting weeds. As the car disappears round the corner, a tiny worm wriggles across a corner of the drive, making squiggly patterns.

# 17 July

A little sparrow spots the worm and swoops down after it. The sparrow lands in the sloppy cement and whizzes past the worm making a long, deep trench. The worm escapes into the long grass. Next door's cat spies the bird and leaps off the fence to catch it. She chases the bird right across the drive, leaving a line of paw prints behind her.

# 18 July

A passing dog chases the cat and leaves even larger prints! When Daddy and Nicola return, the cement has set and the path is a wonderful mixture of paw prints, claw prints, squiggles and lines. Nicola thinks it is fantastic. Even Dad will admit to quite liking the effect. Nicola proudly shows off the driveway to all her friends, because it is the most unusual one ever!

# 19 July

## Molehill Mayhem

Debbie looks out of the kitchen window to see shallow mounds of earth across the lawn. The piles have appeared overnight and Debbie can't imagine what they are. She follows the trail across her garden, along a grass verge and over a wall into a farmer's field. The line crosses the meadow and disappears into the wood. Debbie skips back home to see if her mum knows what the piles of earth are. Mum is flattening the piles with a big spade.

# 20 July

Mum says the culprits are moles. They dig underground at night and come to the surface to make molehills. The tunnels run for miles and there are chambers for storing food. Moles have strong, wide paws and are expert diggers. They eat worms, insects and leaves and they have very poor eyesight. The moles have moved on and the bald patches in the lawn are soon covered in grass, but Debbie checks the lawn every day hoping to catch a glimpse of one. Maybe next year Debbie!

# 21 July

## Clever Miss Snake

Four friends, Fenella Flamingo, Gail Gazelle, Jillie Giraffe and Hetty Hippo are going to their Saturday morning ballet lesson. They are very excited because this is the last rehearsal before tonight's big show. They have had to leave Ziggy Zebra behind because she has a bad cold and has to say in bed. They are feeling a little worried because Ziggy takes care of all the jobs that need doing off stage.

# 22 July

The friends want everything to run smoothly as their families will all be seated in the front row. Miss Snake, the ballet teacher, can see how nervous the four friends are and feels sorry for them. She thinks of a way to get all the jobs running smoothly. Miss Snake tells the class that she needs someone to do some very important jobs, as well as dancing. Each dancer has one small job to do, while the others dance.

# 23 July

They take turns to move the scenery, control the lights, take charge of the curtains and keep the music playing, whilst Miss Snake keeps an eye on the dancing. Everyone is eager to try out new jobs and can't wait for the evening to start. The ballet show is a success and the audience are very impressed with the teamwork once they know a key member is missing. They give the friends an extra round of applause for doing such a good job. Clever Miss Snake!

# 24 July

## Bats and Birds

In the month of July, the sun doesn't set until quite late in the evening. Jodie is wide-awake in bed, even though it is ten o'clock and way past her bedtime. Jodie always likes to listen to the birds twittering away before they settle down to sleep. The birds have quietened down now, but Jodie still doesn't feel tired. Jodie opens the curtains and looks out at the moon. The sky still hasn't darkened completely.

# 25 July

Jodie can just make out a few shadowy creatures flitting round and round the house. This puzzles Jodie because all the birds are asleep. What could they be? Mummy pops her head round the door and is surprised to see Jodie is still awake. Jodie says she can't sleep until the birds go to bed. Mummy looks out of the window and chuckles.

# 26 July

Mum picks a wildlife book from Jodie's bookcase and they read about bats. When it's dark outside, it is easy to mistake bats for birds. Bats are furry and have leathery wings. They are almost blind, but avoid bumping into things by making high-pitched squeaks. The noise bounces off objects and by listening to the echoes the bat can navigate safely. They are nocturnal and they like to hang upside down as they sleep. Jodie is also asleep now. She's upside down too with her feet on the pillow! Mummy tucks her up and kisses her goodnight.

# 27 July

## Princess Poppy

Princess Poppy lives in a grand castle at the top of a steep hill. She is a very lucky little girl because she seems to have everything she could ever wish for. She has rooms full of toys and wardrobes filled with beautiful clothes and shoes. She has her very own hairdresser who is with her every minute of the day, in case a hair strays out of place. She has dozens of personal servants and there is even someone to read books to her!

# 28 July

Princess Poppy should be the happiest little girl in the world, but she is probably the most bored little girl in the world! Looking out of her bedroom window, she sees the cook's three children helping with everyone's chores, down in the yard. They look to be having so much fun. She decides to join them, so she picks out her prettiest dress and daintiest shoes and skips down the stairs to meet them. The children are helping the groom to clean the stables and they are covered in straw and dust.

# 29 July

When Poppy asks if she can join in, they take one look at her pink dress, sparkly shoes and manicured nails and burst out laughing. Poppy turns to go before they see her tears. As she crosses the courtyard, the groom feels sorry for her and hands her a pile of old clothes that he's grown out of. He tells her to come back when she's got changed. Poppy is back five minutes later and this time the children are happy to let her join in.

# 30 July

Poppy is grubby and tired after cleaning the stables and feeding the horses, but she can't remember the last time she enjoyed herself so much. Now Poppy spends a lot of her time helping the groom, the gardener and the cook, or just playing with her new friends. The children also like spending time in Poppy's room, with all her toys and books and they enjoy dressing up in Poppy's fabulous clothes. Poppy thinks it's much more fun to share and she loves being with her new friends.

# 31 July

## Bruno Bear

Bruno Bear collects musical instruments, even though he cannot play any of them. He just enjoys hanging them on the cave walls. Bruno's cave is quite small and because the instruments take up so much room Bruno is worried he may have to get rid of a few. Esther Elephant is coming to tea this afternoon. She's rather large and Bruno is not sure she will fit into his crowded cave.

At 3 o'clock, Esther arrives and squeezes herself into a chair, knocking Bruno's instruments off the wall and flattening them underfoot! She settles down to Bruno's cream buns and coconut milk and, after a lovely tea, waves goodbye to him. Bruno tidies up his flattened instruments with a big smile on his face. He hangs them all up again and they take up much less space. Now he has room for lots more! Every time Bruno wants another musical instrument, he is sure to call Esther over to flatten it before he hangs it on the wall!

# 1 August

## Naughty or Nice

Three year old Fergus is either very good or very naughty. Granny thinks he's as good as gold, but Grandad says he's a bit of a handful. Fergus likes to sit on Granny's knee with a glass of milk and an apple, as she reads stories to him. Grandad gives Fergus a can of pop and a bag of sugary sweets and tries to get Fergus to sit still as he reads a story. It never works! Fergus wriggles and fidgets and usually ends up spilling his drink.

Fergus doesn't know why he behaves so badly, but Mummy does.
She tells Fergus that he has a tiny, well-behaved Fergus sitting on one shoulder and a tiny, badly behaved Fergus on the other. They both try to tell him how to behave. The well-behaved Fergus usually has the loudest voice, but the badly behaved Fergus loves sugary drinks and sweets and these make him much louder. So each time Grandad gives Fergus his sugary treats, he misbehaves! Now Fergus only eats healthy foods and happily sits on Grandad's knee for hours.

# 2 August

**Sherlock Detective Agency**

Sherlock Sheepdog is a very clever dog. The farm animals always call for him when there is a mystery to be solved. One afternoon, as Sherlock dozes in the sunshine, Bertie Blackbird shakes him awake and tells him there is an emergency at the farmhouse. Sherlock leaps into action. He grabs his magnifying glass, binoculars and notebook and races into the house.

# 3 August

Sherlock finds Tom Cat tied to the table leg with a note stuck to his forehead. It reads:

'LEAVE FIVE KILOS OF
BEST CHEESE BY THE
STABLE DOOR OR KITTY CAT
GETS IT!'

Sherlock unties Tom and asks if he recognised any of the kidnappers. Tom shakes his head because it was dark and they all wore masks. Sherlock scans the floor with his magnifying glass. He sees faint paw prints and a few ginger hairs from Kitty.

# 4 August

Sherlock follows the trail across the wooden floor and down the stone steps, into the farmyard. He examines the stables through the binoculars and sees some movement in the rafters. Sherlock creeps over to the stable door and quietly climbs the ladder to the loft. In a dark corner he sees four pairs of eyes frowning at him. Sherlock takes a deep breath and barks as loudly as he can.

# 5 August

Four huge rats squeal as they escape through windows and doors, leaving a very cross Kitty Cat tied up in the straw. Kitty is very pleased to be rescued and shows Sherlock the rats' hoard of stolen goods. There are buns, biscuits, carrots, cakes, pastries and pies. The Farmer is so pleased to be rid of the rats that he lets Sherlock have all the food. Sherlock throws a party for everyone and the animals insist he has the biggest slice of cake.

## Farrah Frog

Farrah Frog has lots of new babies. The babies began life as frogspawn in a woodland pond, before hatching into tiny, black tadpoles. The tadpoles are fat little creatures with wiggly tails but as they get older, the tails disappear and they grow arms and legs. Farrah has twenty-seven babies and she has to choose a name for each of them. She picks one name for each letter of the alphabet.

7 August

Let's see the names she has chosen: Albert, Bella, Clarence, Daryl, Edwin, Fiona, Guy, Heather, Ian, Josie, Kevin, Lana, Michael, Nicole, Oliver, Polly, Quentin, Rachel, Scott, Tessa, Ursula, Victor, Wendy, Xavier, Yasmin and Zach. There is one little baby left, but Farrah can't think of anymore names! She is going to let you choose the last baby's name. Write the name here

................................................

Farrah thinks this is a lovely name!

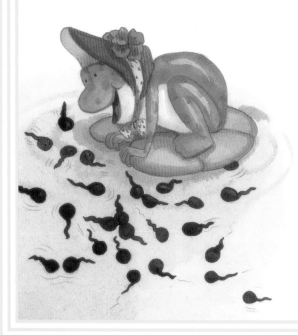

# 8 August

## Granny's Tea

Granny Rabbit is coming for tea today and Mummy Rabbit lets Tim and Tammy make the food all by themselves. Mummy won't let them use the oven or the hotplate, but they can use the microwave. Tammy prepares a salad with lettuce, radishes, carrots and tomatoes from the vegetable patch. Then Tim adds slices of cheese and chunks of Mummy's homemade bread.

# 9 August

For dessert they make chocolate crunchies. They melt pieces of chocolate in the microwave, then pour them into a bowl of cornflakes. Tammy adds slices of banana and Tim stirs until everything is coated in chocolate. He spoons the mixture into bun cases and pops them into the fridge to set. Granny Rabbit says it is the best meal she has had for a long time and she can hardly believe the two little rabbits made it all by themselves.

# 10 August

## The Foolish Flower Fairy

There are hundreds of flower fairies living in the woods near you. They are almost impossible to see, because they disguise themselves so well. Fairy Bluebell has long blue hair, a pretty dress made from bluebell petals and a bluebell hat. You will never see her when she stands still amongst her flowers because she blends in so well.

Fairy Clover is almost invisible too when she stands in her flowers with her clover hat and dress and her pretty pink hair.

# 11 August

However, you might spot Fairy Buttercup. She hates the colour yellow so she has dyed her yellow hair purple, her yellow dress red and her yellow hat black! But she still loves the smell of buttercups so that is where she spends her time. One day, a little girl skips into the wood to pick a posy of flowers for her Granny and immediately sees Fairy Buttercup. She tries to catch her, but the fairy flutters away just in time.

# 12 August

The little girl chases Fairy Buttercup all the way through the wood. The tiny fairy is exhausted and makes one last dash for freedom. She throws herself into a muddy puddle, then curls up next to a pile of stones. It's a perfect disguise. The little girl hunts amongst the leaves and pebbles for a while, then gives up and goes back into the wood to collect her flowers. Fairy Buttercup finds a clean stream to wash out the blue hair dye. She finds a clump of buttercups to make into new yellow clothes. She decides she much prefers yellow after all!

# 13 August

## High In The Sky

Robert is flying to Spain today. He's feeling nervous because he has never been on an aeroplane before. Daddy hauls the suitcases onto the conveyer belt and they disappear through a gap in the wall. They seem to be waiting for ages before it's their turn to board the plane and Robert squirms with excitement! They climb the steps up to the aeroplane. It's enormous! How can this thing fly?

# 14 August

The airhostess sees that Robert is worried and offers to let him meet the pilot after take-off. Robert can't believe his luck. The plane taxies down the runway then speeds up to leave the ground. Robert watches the buildings getting further and further away. The houses are almost too small to be seen. Then suddenly, they are over the sea. It seems to stretch forever! The airhostess comes back and takes him to the cockpit. The captain is very friendly and lets Robert sit in the co-pilot's chair.

# 15 August

The captain has a break while the automatic pilot flies the aeroplane. He tells Robert about the different countries he has flown to and Robert is enthralled. The captain shows Robert how he uses the panel of instruments to fly the plane. Robert asks if he can be a pilot when he grows up. The captain says if he works hard at school and does well in his exams, then he might well become a pilot. Robert has a wonderful holiday in Spain, but the most enjoyable thing for him was definitely the flight.

# 16 August

## Moving House

Stanley and his Mummy stand in the rain at the bottom of the garden and watch the removal men loading furniture into a van. It takes all morning to empty the house, then the family lock the front door and drive away to a new home. The sun starts to shine as another removal van arrives to fill the house with different furniture. The new owners spend the rest of the day dusting and cleaning.

# 17 August

Stanley wonders why the family wants to move. Mummy says the house became too small for the family when they had their third child. Stanley is a garden snail and carries his house on his back. As Stanley grows bigger, so does his house! Mummy and Stanley crawl down the path to a sunny spot. If it rains again, they'll curl up in their shells, all warm and cosy. They don't need umbrellas or new houses. Stanley is glad he's not human!

# ☀ 18 August

## The Zodiac

Jenna is five on the 18th of August and she tells everyone she meets that today is her birthday. The lady at the post office finds a lollypop for her and says Jenna's horoscope looks pretty good. Jenna's glad it looks good but she has no idea what a horoscope is! Mummy explains that it's about the signs of the zodiac.

AQUARIUS
January 20th
– February 18th

PISCES
February 18th – March 20th

ARIES
March 20th –
April 19th

TAURUS
April 20th – May 20th

GEMINI
May 20th – June 20th

# ☀ 19 August

She tells Jenna that there are twelve zodiac signs. Each person's sign depends upon which day they are born. Jenna's birth date comes under Leo the Lion, which means she is a fire sign and is always full of fun. Daddy is a Scorpio, because he is born on November 7th. Jenna doesn't like the scorpion picture much.

## 20 August

Jenna thinks Mummy's sign is cute, it's a goat because Mummy is an Aries, born on April 8th. Jenna likes the horoscope pictures in the newspaper and wants to keep them. Mummy helps her to cut them out and stick them into her scrapbook. Jenna loves drawing and she sits down with her box of crayons and copies her favourite signs onto the next page.

CANCER
June 21st–July 22nd

LEO
July 21st –
August 22nd

VIRGO
August 22nd–
September 22nd

LIBRA
September 22nd
– October 22nd

SCORPIO
October 22nd–
November 21st

SAGITTARIUS
November 22nd
–December 21st

CAPRICORN
December 21st
–January 19th

## 21 August

Newspaper horoscopes tell the reader what might be going to happen to them each day. Although Jenna doesn't actually believe that the horoscopes are true, she still likes Mummy to read hers to her every morning, just for fun. Which sign is your birth date under?

# 22 August

## The Fairground Ballerina

The fair has come to town. Sam and Sally Swan can see the top of the helter-skelter slide, just peeping over the tops of the trees. The two little swans look forward to the annual August fair and have been saving up their pocket money for weeks.

Rides and stalls fill every corner of Farmer Black's field. There are red, yellow and blue flashing lights and gaily coloured flags, waving in the breeze. The rich aroma of candyfloss, toffee apples and hotdogs is in the air.

# 23 August

As they pass the hoopla stall, Sally sees a beautiful ballerina doll amongst the prizes. Her jet black hair is tied up with flowers and her pretty pink tutu is studded with sequins. Sally longs to win her, so she pays for twelve hooplas. She tries so hard to throw a ring over the ballerina, but misses every time. Sally spends all her money and has nothing left for anything else. She trails after Sam as he bumps his car round the dodgems, rides the painted carousel horses and slides down the enormous helter-skelter.

# 24 August

Sam offers his candyfloss to Sally to cheer her up, but she can only think about the doll. Before they leave the fair, Sally goes back for one last look at it. In front of the stall, half hidden in the grass, Sally sees a fat wallet. It is bulging with money. Sally sees the stallholder frantically searching for his wallet amongst the hooplas. She immediately hands the wallet over. He is so grateful that he tells Sally to choose anything she likes from his stall. Guess what she chooses? Sam and Sally have had a wonderful day.

# 25 August

## Clever Old Harrold

No one can remember a time when Harold Hare wasn't around and no one knows just how old he is, not even Harold himself! He has become very forgetful in his old age, so the neighbours like to keep a friendly eye on him. They take his washing in when it rains. They turn off his oven when he forgets to take his food out. They bring him home when he forgets where he lives. The neighbours are all very fond of Harold, but he is sad because he feels he's a bit of a nuisance to them.

# 26 August

One morning, Harold wheels out his shopping trolley and catches the bus to town. He has a long list of things to buy from the supermarket. He withdraws some money from the cash point outside the bank and then potters down the street to the shops, leaving his trolley on the steps of the bank!

Inside the bank, three masked robbers are stealing all the money. The bank doors burst open and the robbers race down the steps to their getaway car.

# 27 August

A burly robber crashes into the shopping trolley and tumbles down the steps, knocking down the other two. They land in a tangled pile, as forgetful Harold returns for his trolley. The police arrive just as he is tugging it out from underneath the bank robbers. Everyone congratulates Harold and calls him a hero. The local paper prints a lovely story about him and his neighbours are very proud. Harold doesn't think he's hero at all, but he does feel just a little bit more important and that makes him very happy indeed.

## 28 August

### Garden Bath Time

'You all need a good bath!' says Mummy as Mishka the German shepherd dog pads across the kitchen floor, followed by two grubby children and three sets of footprints. The children grumble so much about having a bath that Mummy thinks of a clever way to clean them up. She fills a bucket full of water and asks Jack and Gemma to wash the dog outside in the garden. Mishka soon disappears under a blanket of foam.

## 29 August

Mishka stands patiently while the children take turns rinsing off the bubbles with a hosepipe. A beautifully clean dog now stands next to two grubby children, but Mummy isn't too worried as she knows what will happens next. Mishka gives herself an enormous shake. It starts at her head and works its way down to her tail. Water flies off in all directions and the children are completely soaked - and clean! Mission accomplished!

# 30 August

## Pixie in a Pocket

Pixie is Sean's pet gerbil. He's rather like a big mouse, with huge back legs. Sean plays with Pixie in his bedroom for half an hour each day before breakfast. Pixie is being naughty today and won't go back into his cage. Sean looks all around his bedroom but can't find Pixie, not even in the bookcase where he likes chewing books. He's hiding in Sean's jacket pocket. After breakfast, Sean pulls his jacket on and heads off to Tim's house.

# 31 August

Pixie peeps over the edge of Sean's pocket and the sun warms his face as he watches the birds and butterflies in the sky and the fast cars on the road. He really enjoys the journey until they arrive at Tim's house. Tim owns four cats! As soon as they smell Pixie they jump up at Sean. Sean wonders what they want and digs around his pocket pulling out a terrified little gerbil. Pixie wants to be back in his cosy little cage so Sean tucks him up safely and runs back home with him. Silly Pixie!

 # 1 September

## Moving House

September is a busy month for Fred the farmer. Fred spends long days harvesting his crops and haymaking. Harvey the Harvest Mouse and his wife, Helga, have built their tiny nest in Fred's cornfield, along with many other mice. September is the month that Fred cuts the corn with his combine harvester. Harvey can hear the horrid machine as it ploughs up and down the field getting nearer and nearer to their home.

 # 2 September

Helga begs Harvey to leave, but he's far too stubborn. Streams of neighbours rush past their nest clutching their children.

The combine harvester is very close now. The ground trembles and the noise is deafening. Helga can see gleaming red metal as it cuts a tract through the corn, only inches away from them. With only seconds to spare, Harvey agrees to move.

## 3 September

### The Good Luck Charm

As Fairy Tinks flutters over a stream, she spies something really special on the bank. It's a four-leaf clover. She picks the leaf and pins it to her belt knowing it should bring her good luck all day long. Above her a nasty black crow spots Tinks' pretty wings and thinks she'd be good to eat! He swoops down with open beak and just as he's about to scoop her up she leans forward to adjust the clover and the crow skims over her head and crashes into the water!

## 4 September

Tinks doesn't notice a thing as she flutters across the grass. The clover has become loose in her belt and it slips out. Tinks dives to the ground to catch it, just as the bedraggled crow reaches out for her with his bony claws. He misses once again and crashes into a tree! Tinks still hasn't notice the horrid bird. She sees a group of children playing with fishing nets and flies over to see what they have caught. They are catching butterflies and putting them in a big jam-jar. This makes Tinks really cross.

# 5 September

She wrestles with the lid of the jam-jar but she's not strong enough to pull it off. Behind her the angry crow is racing up to catch her in his sharp beak. He's just about to close his beak on her when she slides off the jam-jar lid and lands on the grass. The unlucky crow rams his beak into the lid and is stuck fast. He shakes and bangs the lid until it falls to the ground. The butterflies escape and the crow decides that chasing fairies is far too dangerous.

# 6 September

Tinks feels sorry for the battered and bruised crow. He looks like he's had a really bad day. She offers him the four-leaf clover saying, 'I think you should have this. It's supposed to bring luck although I can't say I've noticed anything different today!' She lays it on his knee and flies away. The grumpy crow flicks the leaf away. It catches the breeze and pokes him in the eye! I think it only works if you are nice!

 **7 September**

### Dippy Diplodocus

Dippy Diplodocus is a very sensible dinosaur. His two best friends, Stiggy Stegosaurus and Tilly Triceratops are always finding themselves in trouble and teasing Dippy for not joining in. Today they are having a picnic at the edge of the forest. They are not allowed to go inside, because scary dinosaurs like Tyrannosaurus Rex live in there.

When Tilly kicks the ball into the trees she and Stiggy race into the forest to find it.

**8 September**

Dippy calls them back but they pay no attention and soon find themselves deep in the forest. The massive trees tower far above their heads, blotting out most of the sky and they realise the ball is well and truly lost. And so are they!

Just ahead, the trees appear to thin out so Stiggy and Tilly squeeze between the massive trunks and burst into a clearing. They flop down on a pile of rocks and hope someone comes to find them soon.

# 9 September

As they wait, they hear the sound of heavy footsteps in the distance. They are coming closer and closer every second and the ground shakes with the force of them. There is only one beast capable of so much noise. It's the terrifying Tyrannosaurus Rex! Stiggy and Tilly dive under the rocks just as T. Rex strides over their hiding place.

'Oh why won't someone rescue us?' sobs Tilly.

# 10 September

At the edge of the forest, Dippy watches as T. Rex thunders through the trees. He waits until he's long gone and then shouts loudly for his friends. Stiggy and Tilly's mums hear Dippy calling and come to help but the trees are too thick to see through. Then Dippy has an idea, he stands the two mums together and climbs onto their backs. Dippy has such a long neck that he can see over the tops of the trees and his friends can see him. He guides them back to safety and they get a strict telling off. Clever Dippy. I don't think they'll tease him anymore!

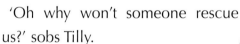

# 11 September

## Lost At Sea

Jason and Martha take an inflatable dinghy to the beach. Mum and Dad let them play in it as long as they stay at the edge of the shore and don't float out to sea. The breaking waves toss the little dinghy up and down and the children pretend they are pirates, sailing a stormy ocean. They don't notice the tide gently pulling them out to sea. Martha sees how far they have drifted and starts to panic.

# 12 September

Jason hugs her but he worries too when he sees a large triangular fin steadily approaching the dinghy. Jason has read about sharks and can imagine row upon row of sharp white teeth. The fin sinks below the water and seconds later a large grey head, with a friendly smile pops up beside them. It's a dolphin! Jason has read about dolphins too. They are intelligent creatures that are renown for helping sailors lost at sea.

# 13 September

The dolphin nudges the dinghy toward the shore with its beak. They bump onto the sand and the dolphin splashes back out to sea. Dad is engrossed in a newspaper and Mum is sunbathing with her eyes closed. No one noticed they were gone! As they drag the dinghy back up the beach, the children decide never to use the dinghy unless Mum or Dad are keeping a very close eye on them.

# 14 September

## Best of Friends

Rex enjoys life. He takes his human, Bert, into the garden and lies in the sun while Bert digs happily amongst the flowers. At five o'clock it will be time to take Bert for a walk. Bert is quite old now, but Rex gives him three good walks each day. Rex has spent a lot of time training his human. Bert walks well on the lead and knows how to throw balls and sticks. Rex is very fond of Bert. They have been together for a long time. He knows that man is a dog's best friend. He gives Bert a friendly pat then they both close their eyes and doze in the afternoon sunshine.

# 15 September

## Nosy Mrs Parker

Mrs Parker doesn't have many friends and so she's become a little bit nosy. You can often see her hovering behind the net curtains, keeping a close eye on what's going on. The neighbours are annoyed at her curiosity and tend to ignore her.

One morning, as Mrs Parker sits at the kitchen window, a removal van parks outside the Tomkin's house. Two men start to load up the van with the Tomkin's furniture.

# 16 September

There is no 'for sale' sign outside the house and as she hasn't seen the Tomkins for nearly a week, she thinks they must be on holiday. Mrs Parker is very concerned and decides to call the police. As the patrol car rounds the corner, the two men drop the sofa and try to run away. They leap over the fence into Mrs Parker's garden. As they land, Mrs Parker knocks them on the head with her umbrella, so they jump back over the fence and into the arms of the police!

# 17 September

The burglars are arrested and all the neighbours get together to move the furniture back into the house.

When the Tomkins return from their holiday and hear about the burglars they invite Mrs Parker round for tea to thank her. Mrs Parker's neighbours always tell her when they are going away now and she keeps an eye on their houses. She has made a lot of new friends and won't ever be lonely again!

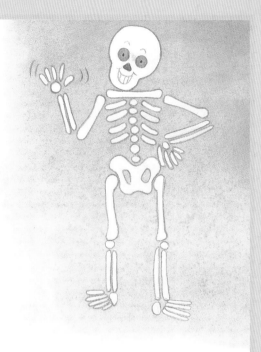

# 18 September

## The Skeleton

Shane is digging the garden with Daddy when he unearths a small piece of bone. Daddy thinks it could part of a mouse skeleton. Shane is fascinated and wants to know more about his own bones. Daddy finds a book about the human body and flicks through it to find a diagram of the skeleton. Shane looks at the picture for ages until he has learned the names of some of the main bones, then he draws a skeleton and labels it to show Daddy. Daddy is very impressed.

# 19 September

## Greedy Ghost

Peter's granny lives in a house that is over two hundred years old. It's a house with a lot of history and Peter loves exploring the old-fashioned rooms, dark, dusty cellars and the cluttered, cobwebbed attic. Peter's two brothers tease him with scary ghost stories, but they don't worry Peter. Today he has a mystery to solve. A tub of strawberry ice cream vanished from Granny's fridge yesterday morning, a packet of biscuits went missing last night and a huge slice of chocolate cake disappeared from the pantry this morning!

# 20 September

Peter makes a list of the missing items and goes down for breakfast. Granny leaves two slices of buttered toast on Peter's plate while he is pouring a glass of milk. But when Peter sits at the table there is only half a slice of toast left! What's going on? Peter decides to set a trap. He secretly makes a tasty looking sandwich, thickly spread with mustard and extra hot chilli peppers. He leaves the sandwich on the kitchen table and turns away to wash the dishes.

# 21 September

When he looks back, the plate is empty! Peter's brothers are kicking a ball about in the garden, so they haven't eaten it. Granny is quietly reading the paper and sipping a cup of tea, so she hasn't eaten it. Peter is puzzled. He runs upstairs to clean his teeth and hears someone coughing and spluttering in the bathroom. He pulls open the door, catching the food thief still holding half the sandwich.

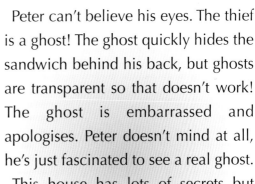

# 22 September

Peter can't believe his eyes. The thief is a ghost! The ghost quickly hides the sandwich behind his back, but ghosts are transparent so that doesn't work! The ghost is embarrassed and apologises. Peter doesn't mind at all, he's just fascinated to see a real ghost.

This house has lots of secrets but Peter's secret is the best. He keeps his ghostly friend supplied with sandwiches and, in return, the ghost tells Peter the many secrets he knows about the house.

## 23 September

### The Forgetful Ladybird

Larry and Libby Ladybird are having a race. The first to reach Aunty Linda's house wins. Libby takes one path and Larry takes another. Libby is very forgetful and can never remember the fastest way to get to Aunty Linda's. She climbs Molehill Mountain, skirts around the pit in the middle and slides down the other side into dense forest. Keeping one eye on the sun to guide her, she soon reaches the steep sides of a large, water-filled crater and scrambles to the top.

## 24 September

Dog Bowl Lake is quite close to Aunty Linda's and she thinks she'll make it before nightfall. A stray leaf makes a perfect boat to cross the lake and at the other side she slides down Spade Handle Hill and races the last few steps to Number Three, Geranium Row. Aunty Linda is waiting with a mug of hot chocolate and to her surprise so is Larry! 'How did you get here so quickly?' she asks. 'I flew,' says Larry. 'Silly me,' says Libby. 'I forgot I have wings!' What a forgetful ladybird she is!

# 25 September

## Percy and Penny

Percy and Penny are homing pigeons. They live in a loft and are well looked after by Philip. On race days Philip gently packs the two pigeons in a box and drives them miles and miles away from home and then releases them. Percy and Penny are very clever at finding their way back home. They use the earth's magnetic field to navigate and find their way home, even if they have been released thousands of miles away! Percy knows a lot about his ancestors.

# 26 September

Some were owned by famous historical people, like Julius Caesar, who used them to send messages to his troops in times of war. In more recent times, pilots would carry homing pigeons in their aircraft and release them if they were shot down during wartime. The pigeons would fly home and help would soon be on its way. Percy and Penny are nearly home. They can see their cosy pigeon loft in the distance. Philip will have fresh food and water waiting for them. It's good to be home.

# 27 September

## Maurice and the Cheese Monsters

Maurice Mouse is a scientist and his latest project is to find out if the moon is really made of cheese. He plans an expedition to test it for himself. Maurice climbs into his rocket: 10.. 9.. 8.. 7.. 6.. 5.. 4.. 3.. 2.. 1.. BLAST OFF!

Maurice shoots into space. He's on his way. Then he gently touches down on the moon's bright yellow surface.

# 28 September

Maurice takes a long deep sniff and the wonderful aroma of fresh cheese fills his nostrils. He takes out a knife and cuts a large slice out of the moon. It tastes delicious! Suddenly shouts and screams fill the air and hoards of cheese monsters race towards him. They're angry because Maurice is eating their moon! Maurice leaps for the rocket's ladder and scrambles up the rungs as fast as he can, but the cheese monsters catch him and shake him until he falls off.

# 29 September

Maurice thumps to the ground with a cheese monster still gripping his leg. But when he opens his eyes, he sees Mummy standing with a plate in one hand and his leg in the other! She says, 'Wake up Maurice, it's supper time!' Maurice must have been dreaming. He chuckles to himself and curls up on the sofa to enjoy a slice of cheese on toast. From the sofa, Maurice can see the moon in the night sky. It's crescent shaped. In fact, it rather looks as if someone has taken a bite out of it!

# 30 September

## The Old Oak Tree

Joe sits at the bottom of his garden and stares thoughtfully at an old oak tree. Daddy says it is about 700 hundred years old. Joe thinks of all that's happened around this ancient, gnarled tree. When it was young, people travelled past on horseback. As it grew older, they raced past in trains and cars. Then they flew over it in aeroplanes. Now, astronauts can fly high above the tree and out into space! Joe wishes the tree could talk, what wonderful tales it would tell.

# 1 October

## Wait And See

One morning, Parrot flies to Lion's den and asks if she could have a clawful of strong hairs from his mane.

'Of course you can,' says Lion. 'But what do you want them for?'

'Wait and see,' says Parrot.

Then Parrot flies into Bear's cave and asks him if she could have a clawful of straw and dried leaves from his cave floor.

'Of course you can,' says Bear. 'But what do you want them for?'

'Wait and see,' says Parrot.

# 2 October

Next, Parrot flies to Flamingo's pond and asks if she could have a beakful of soft pink feathers.

'Of course you can,' says Flamingo. 'But what do you want them for?'

'Wait and see,' says Parrot.

The next day, Parrot invites Lion, Bear and Flamingo for tea. When the three friends arrive at Parrot's tree they see why she asked for all those things. Parrot has made a beautiful new nest, which is strong, warm and just right for her two newborn chicks. 'Now you know what I wanted everything for!' laughs Parrot.

# 3 October

## Woodland Cleanup

There is a wood near Dominic's house that used to be really pretty but is now full of litter. The woodland path is lined with empty cans, cigarette ends, sweet wrappers and plastic bags. Dominic never drops litter anywhere other than in a bin and he wishes everyone else would do the same. Dominic's mum suggests he forms a cleanup group with his classmates to tidy the wood. Dominic's teacher likes the idea and arranges a day in the wood for the class. Everyone is issued with rubber gloves and a large bin liner.

# 4 October

The class work their way through the trees picking up rubbish as they go. Dominic's teacher keeps a close eye on her pupils and tells them what to remove and what to leave. At the end of the day they have thirty bags full of litter and a very tidy wood. The local newspaper hears about their efforts. They take photos of the wood and the children and write a wonderful article about the cleanup. The Mayor presents the school with an award and the local council provides two litterbins for the wood. Dominic is very happy now. The wood is litter free and pretty once again. Clever Dominic!

# 5 October

## The Magic Garden

Old Mrs Perkins has an absolutely fantastic ornamental garden. There is a pretty goldfish pond that is surrounded by ceramic frogs, red and white spotted toadstools, assorted gnomes, a tiny windmill and a tall, plastic heron. Some of the gnomes stand amid the flowerbeds, whilst others perch on toadstools or pose with their fishing rods around the pond. Maya and Jake can see Mrs Perkins' house from their bedroom window and have noticed something rather strange about her garden.

# 6 October

Each day the gnomes seem to change position. Yesterday Jake noticed the gnome with the red hat perched upon a toadstool, but today the same gnome is fishing by the windmill! Maya is quite sure the heron by the bird table was standing in the middle of the pond yesterday! Maya and Jake have a plan to see if Mrs Perkins is moving the ornaments around at night or if the ornaments are moving about by themselves. It's dark outside now and the children are tucked up in bed.

# 7 October

Mummy and Daddy think Maya and Jake are asleep but they are wide-awake and waiting for the lights to go out in Mrs Perkins' house. Before bedtime, the children drew a rough plan of the garden showing the positions of all the ornaments. At midnight Jake looks out of his bedroom window. The street lamps light up the garden and Jake can see that everything is in the same place. He watches for two hours before waking Maya. They take turns all night, but still nothing happens.

# 8 October

Soon it is time to get up. The two exhausted children drag themselves out of bed. Disappointed, they eat their breakfasts and set off to school, taking one last look at Mrs Perkins' garden as they pass. Nothing has changed and Jake wonders if they just imagined everything. But as they disappear around the bend, Mrs Perkins opens her front door and claps her hands three times. The ornaments burst into life, race round the garden to new positions and then change back into ornaments.

Mrs Perkins chuckles and goes back inside her house with her black cat!

## 9 October

### The Colourful Chameleon

It's Carly Chameleon's birthday and she has lots of presents to open. Sitting amongst the green leaves in her tree, Carly is a lovely green colour too. But as she picks up her first present, she turns red to match the paper. When she holds the yellow ribbon, she turns yellow. The same happens with the pink, blue and purple presents. Chameleons are very clever at camouflaging themselves by colouring their skin to match their surroundings. But watch out when Carly's skin turns dark, because that means she is cross and she might stick her very, very long tongue out at you!

## 10 October

### School Holidays

Stuart is a bit bored during the school holidays, because most of the children in his class have gone away for the week. Stuart's family can't go on holiday because the builders are here to extend their kitchen and Daddy wants to be around to help. A big lorry dumps an enormous mound of sand on the driveway next to a pile of bricks. Stuart makes sandcastles while his Daddy talks to the workmen.

# 11 October

One of the builders asks Stuart to pass him a brick. Stuart has to put a yellow hard hat on before taking the brick to the man. Stuart likes helping and Daddy says it's okay as long as he stays close to him, because building sites can be dangerous. Building a wall looks hard work so Stuart goes to the kitchen and pours orange squash for the three men. Over the next few days, the extension quickly takes shape and Stuart is disappointed when the holiday ends and he has to go back to school.

# 12 October

At school, the children take turns to tell the class what they did during the holiday. Some children have been abroad, some have visited relatives and some have gone to play schemes for the week. When it's Stuart's turn he describes the extension, the machines, the workmen and how he helped with odd jobs. Stuart thinks his holiday was by far the most fun and he even thinks he might like to be a builder when he grows up.

# 13 October

## The Conker Contest

Sukie Squirrel has collected hundreds of acorns and stored them in a hole at the bottom of her oak tree. Acorns are Sukie's favourite food and she needs a lot of them to get her through the lean winter months. As Sukie sorts through the nuts, throwing away all the bad ones, she keeps finding strange round nuts covered in spikes. She has quite a lot of these and wonders if they taste good. Peeling off the green, spiky outer case, Sukie finds a hard, brown nut inside that she cannot bite into. So she tosses the nuts into the long grass.

# 14 October

When two young weasels scamper past Sukie's tree, they come across the unwanted nuts and can't believe their luck. They scour the forest floor for bits of discarded string, then tie the nuts to the string. Sukie is very curious so the weasles tell her they are going to play 'conkers'. They take turns hitting each other's conker until one of them splits. The winner is the owner of the unbroken conker. Sukie wants to play and so do all the other forest creatures, so the weasles hold a contest. The winner is Tommy Toad, with seven wins and the contest is so popular that they decide to hold it every year.

### Night Monsters

Jasmine snores gently. She and Teddy are cosily tucked up in her nice, warm bed on this chilly October night. An owl hoots as it flies past her window and the noise wakes her up with a start. Jasmine's night lamp has been turned off and the only light in the room comes from the pale moon shining through half closed curtains. The once familiar bedroom now seems full of unfriendly objects. Jasmine stares in horror at a monstrous shape, which has appeared at the foot of her bed.

Jasmine clutches Teddy and cowers behind the duvet as the monster fades into the shadows, leaving wide staring eyes. In a moment of bravery, Jasmine reaches out and punches the switch on the night lamp. Light floods the room and Jasmine finds herself face to face with .........THE MIRROR!

The wide staring eyes were hers. She scribbles a note and props it against her night lamp. It reads:

PLEASE NEVER, EVER TURN MY
NIGHT LIGHT OFF,
(OR AT LEAST NOT UNTIL I'M
SIX), LOVE  JASMINE XXX

# 17 October

## Salt and Pepper

Salt and Pepper are two little mice who live next door to each other in Daisy Wood. Salt is a very kind mouse, but Pepper is a very selfish mouse. One chilly October morning the two mice are playing together in the wood when old Mrs Badger pokes her head out of her doorway and asks the mice to nip down to the farm to collect some fresh milk and eggs for her. Pepper says the farm is too far away and refuses to go, but kind hearted Salt sets off immediately. It will take hours to get there, so Mrs Badger gives him a sandwich and a bottle of water to take with him.

# 18 October

By lunchtime Salt is very hungry and sits on a stone at the side of the track to eat his sandwich. He notices a tired old rabbit slowly making her way up the track towards him. The old rabbit gazes longingly at the food as she shuffles past. Salt feels sorry for her and offers to share the food. The old rabbit is delighted and sits down next to Salt. Once they have eaten, the old rabbit leaps to her feet and throws off her furry coat, revealing herself to be a little fairy. The fairy waves her magic wand and a large wheelbarrow appears, piled high with food. The food is for Salt for being so kind. Salt thanks the fairy and runs back home pushing the wheelbarrow. Salt shares the food with all the woodland creatures. Pepper is very jealous of Salt's good fortune, so the very next day he sets off down the same track.

# 19 October

After a while, Pepper sees a duck sitting on the path with an injured foot. As he walks past, the duck asks if he will help her to get back to her pond. The detour will take Pepper well away from the road and Pepper wants to find the old rabbit that turns into a fairy, so he refuses to help and goes on his way. As he starts to leave, the duck jumps to her feet and shakes off her feathers to reveal a cross little fairy. The fairy waves her wand and a wheelbarrow full of wonderful food appears. Pepper is delighted and races back home without even saying thank you. As Pepper gets closer to home he notices the food beginning to rot.

# 20 October

By the time he reaches his front door, the food smells dreadful and all the neighbours hold their noses and tell him to throw it away. As Pepper gets rid of the food, he realises what a selfish mouse he's been. He decides to be kinder from now on. The fairy watches Pepper and thinks that he's learned his lesson. She leaves a tasty red apple on his doorstep and flies away. When Pepper sees it on his step, he cuts it in two and shares it with Salt because that's what friends do!

# 21 October

## A Lazy Afternoon

One hot day in sunny South Africa, a fat bee buzzes around a little lion cub called Amber. Amber is dozing in the long grass and flicks her tail to shoo the bee away. But it just won't go. Amber opens one eye and debates whether it's worth chasing the annoying bee. Then the bee lands on Amber's nose and begins to clean itself. Amber swats at the insect with her paw and scratches her nose. She leaps up and tries to catch the bee, but it's too quick for her and she ends up chasing the silly insect all around the other sleeping lions.

# 22 October

When Amber barges into her dad, a huge, brown lion with a magnificent mane, he leaps to his feet and roars so loudly that Amber's ears ring! Then she clambers over her sleeping mum, races around the tree and finally collapses, exhausted, on top of her brother and sister. Dad is always very grumpy if he's woken up and Mum is annoyed that Amber has disturbed the two younger cubs. Amber is ordered to lie down by the acasia tree and not move until suppertime. The bee zigzags across the grass and laughs at Amber as she flops down in the shade, sighing noisily.

# 23 October

The annoying bee is gaily doing somersaults over Amber's head and buzzing so loudly that Amber knows she won't be able to fall asleep. Then Amber hears another buzzing noise and sees an enormous Queen Bee homing in on the smaller one. The little bee was supposed to be collecting pollen to make honey for the Queen. Not teasing little lion cubs. Amber watches in amusement as the two bees make lots of angry noises and bang into each other. Then the Queen Bee escorts the naughty little bee back to their hive. Amber snuggles down in the dry grass, with a smile on her face and thinks maybe it's not such a bad day after all.

# 24 October

**A Very Rainy Day**

It has been raining all day and Jenny is very bored. She has read all her library books and done four jigsaw puzzles. She watches the rain through the window and cuddles her dog, Bess. Two little ducks waddle down the road. They're splashing in and out of all the puddles and having a great time. Jenny sees her raincoat and boots and thinks there is no good reason why she shouldn't enjoy the rain too. She buttons up her coat, pulls on her boots and chases Bess into the garden. They play for hours and when they finally come in for tea, Jenny can't help hoping it pours down tomorrow too.

## 25 October

### Percy To The Rescue

Percy Pelican lives at the seaside and hunts for fish every day. Other sea birds fish in the ocean too. Gordon Gull and his noisy friends always seem to be chasing the same fish as Percy. He doesn't like the gulls much, because they are rude and make fun of his enormous, bucket-like beak. One afternoon, as Percy is fishing, he hears Gordon's gang screeching even louder than usual. Percy has a beak full of tasty fish and can't wait to get home for supper, but he's worried that the gulls are in trouble.

## 26 October

Percy turns around and swoops down to the huddle of birds below. Percy knows that if he lands in the water carrying so many fish it will be impossible to take off again. But when he sees Gordon nursing a broken wing he wants to help. The other gulls try to lift Gordon up, but he's too heavy. Percy drops his fish, scoops Gordon up in his beak and flies back home. Gordon is ashamed of his bad behaviour and promises to be kinder from now on and Percy thinks it is well worth losing his supper, because he has made a new friend.

## 27 October

### Lion's New Hair-Do

Lion needs a haircut. His fringe is so long that he can barely see through it. Sitting in the hairdressing salon, Lion flicks through the magazines and tries to pick a style. There are too many to choose from so Lion asks the other customers to decide. Crocodile thinks a curly perm would be rather nice.

'No, no,' says Cheetah. 'Short back and sides is much better!'

## 28 October

Snake thinks a punk hair-do would be perfect, but Elephant wants him to try a bouffant look.

'What about pigtails?' asks Boar.

'Or a pony tail?' suggests Zebra.

'I really can't decide,' Lion says to the hairdresser. 'I think I'll leave it up to you.' He squeezes his eyes tightly shut and lets the hairdresser snip away at his mane. Ten minutes later, Lion opens his eyes and is delighted with the cut. The hairdresser has just tidied up his hair with a trim. Very nice Lion!

 # 29 October

## The Big Party

Marvin Monzta has a rather unusual home. His family live in a tumbledown castle that sits on top of a wooded hill, high above the village. Tonight, Marvin is throwing a party for all his school friends. Although the guests are nervous about visiting the spooky castle, they all want to go to the party because Marvin is such a fun friend to have. He's very different from all the other children in the village.

 # 30 October

Most people have pet dogs and cats, but Marvin has pet worms and bats! Most people travel by bus or car, but Marvin usually arrives in a dusty, black coach pulled by wild, black stallions! Most people wear anoraks or jackets, but Marvin wears a long, black cloak with a rich red lining! And most people like feeding the ducks in the park, but Marvin likes feeding the bats in the dark!

# 31 October

At seven o'clock, the guests knock on the heavy wooden doors and wait as bats and owls circle overhead. A solemn butler, holding a flickering candle, creaks open the door and points them in the direction of the ballroom. The corridors are draped in cobwebs and mice scuttle across the dusty floorboards. Portraits of bygone ancestors glower down at them from ancient frames, as they tiptoe past, huddled together and wide-eyed with anticipation.

The ballroom doors slowly open as the children approach. Coffins and gravestones lean against the walls. Skeletons and broomsticks hang from the ceiling, amongst dusty cobwebs. A giant cauldron occupies the centre of the room and in front of it stands a black cat and Marvin holding a big book of spells. The children are dumbstruck. Suddenly Marvin yells, 'HAPPY HALLOWEEN EVERYONE!' and the fancy dress party begins. It is the best Halloween Party ever!

 # 1 November

## Little Dizzy

Hattie Hadrosaur sits on her nest, waiting for her six large, leathery eggs to hatch. Over the next two days, five baby hadrosaurs emerge, but one egg remains intact. Hattie is very busy looking after her new babies and finds it harder and harder to spend time sitting on the last egg.

 # 2 November

One morning, whilst Hattie is playing with her babies, a greedy pteranodon swoops down and steals the last egg. The egg is heavy and the pteranodon can't fly very far with it. Eventually, the egg slips out of her claws and tumbles through the air, landing in the branches of a fir tree. Down below, a triceratops trundles over to the tree and scratches his back on the rough bark.

# 3 November

The tree shakes violently and the egg wobbles free, bouncing into the long grass. A herd of long necked brontosaurs see the egg rolling towards them and play football with it. They kick the egg around the cliff top, until the smallest brontosaurus accidentally kicks it over the cliff edge. The egg crashes down the slope and splashes into a fast flowing river.

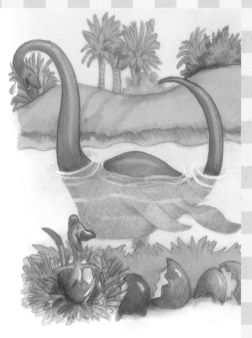

# 4 November

A plesiosaur swims to the egg and flicks it out of the water with her strong tail. The bruised and battered egg flies through the air to land with a satisfying 'plop', back in Hattie's nest, just as she returns with her babies. Then the egg starts to move, all by itself. Suddenly the shell breaks and a tiny, wobbly baby struggles out. The baby is none the worse for his adventure, but he does look a little dizzy. So that's what Hattie decides to call him - Little Dizzy!

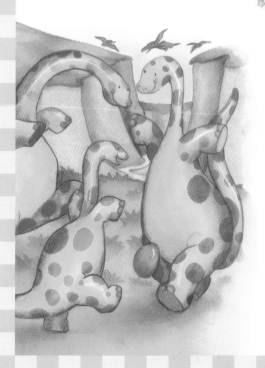

# 5 November

## Simon's First Train Journey

Daddy and Simon are going to visit Granny. She lives miles away, in the city. So they are travelling by train. Simon has never been on a train before. He runs onto the platform, dragging Daddy by the hand. The railway station is packed with people and Daddy holds on tight to Simon. He doesn't want to lose him in the crowd.

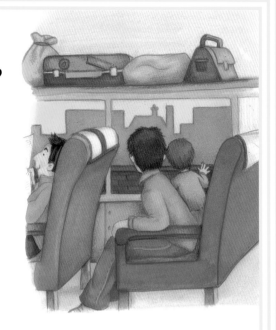

# 6 November

Daddy shows Simon their tickets and points out the seat numbers. Then he lets Simon find the right carriage and they climb on board. The train travels so fast that the countryside blurs into a stream of colour. They whiz through big towns and pretty villages, past ugly factories and wasteland, by farm animals and patchwork fields full of crops. All the time, the train has a wonderful rhythm of its own: Chuggity-chug, chuggity-chug, chuggity-chug.

# 7 November

Simon's eyelids feel heavy and he soon falls asleep. Finally, the train slows down as it approaches the city station and Simon wakes up. The journey seems to have taken no time at all. Granny is waiting for them outside the ticket barrier and Simon rushes over to tell her all about his exciting journey.

'Perhaps you'll be a train driver when you're a grown up,' Granny says with a smile. Simon can't wait!

# 8 November

### Ice Scream

Gemma's big sister is taking her ice-skating today. Gemma has often watched her sister competing, but this is the first time she has tried it herself. The big boots seem clumsy and heavy, but as soon as they touch the ice Gemma feels as if she's floating. Her sister holds her tightly as they glide around the rink and Gemma squeals with laughter. After an hour they are tired and ready to leave, but first they have one last treat. Gemma's sister buys her a big chocolate cornet. 'It's an *ice scream* for my very noisy little sister!' she laughs.

**9 November**

### Freddy Fire Engine

Freddy is a handsome, shiny fire engine who loves his job. Usually, Freddy is very busy putting out house fires and rescuing people and animals from blazing buildings or tall trees. But this morning, Freddy is bored because there is nothing to do. He stares out of the fire station window at the cold, wet streets and decides to motor around the village to see if any of his friends are about.

 **10 November**

The streets are empty and the cars are tucked away in their cosy, warm garages. The only sign of life is a group of school children and their parents, gathered alongside the river. The heavy rain over the past few days has swollen the river so much that in places it has burst its banks. The only way to get the children to school is to cross the river using the little bridge.

# 11 November

Although the river is calm today, the bridge is still partially submerged and no one wants to wade through the muddy waters. Freddy feels sorry for the children and wants to help them. He lowers his ladder to the ground so that two little boys and their Daddy can climb onto the rungs. They sit down, holding on tightly, and very slowly Freddy extends the ladder all the way across the river to the path on the other side.

Then Freddy retracts the ladder and takes the next family over.

# 12 November

Half an hour later, everybody is safely on their way to school. At four o' clock, Freddy is back at the riverbank to transport everyone safely across once more. Freddy has saved the day and he's really enjoyed himself. It always feels nice to do a good turn. He drives back to the fire station with a broad smile on his face.

## Mumbo Jumbo's Mixed-Up Spells

Like most dragons, Mumbo Jumbo can do magic. Unlike most dragons, Mumbo gets dreadfully muddled up when he recites a spell and they always go wrong. The fairy folk rely on dragons to help them out with their special spells, so dragons are usually kept very busy. Except for Mumbo. No one asks him for help after his last two disastrous spells.

# 14 November

Last week, a pixie asked for a spell for a new hat and Mumbo had given him a blue cat. Yesterday, a fairy asked for a gold wand but ended up standing in a cold pond!

Mumbo is close to tears when Mummy Dragon gives him a small blue box, which she hopes will cheer him up. Inside the box is a pair of spectacles. When Mumbo puts them on he can read the spell book perfectly! No more mistakes! Now Mumbo Jumbo is the busiest dragon in the village.

 **15** November

## Stone Age Adventure

Maku is seven years old. His family share a cave with four other families. Maku is the youngest of three brothers and longs to be old enough to join his father and older brothers on hunting trips. Instead, he has to stay at home with his mother, gathering wood for the communal fire. He watches enviously as the hunting party leaves, scrambling down the hillside armed with long spears.

**16** November

The women crowd around the fire and no-one notices when Maku quietly slips away. He follows the men at a safe distance as they cross the valley floor, tracking a herd of hairy mammoths. These gigantic beasts, with their enormous curving tusks, are ancestors of modern day elephants. One mammoth will provide enough meat to feed the families for many weeks and its fur will keep them warm throughout the harsh winter.

# 17 November

From behind a tree, Maku watches as the men separate a mammoth from its herd and close in. But Maku is not the only observer. Across the valley a sinister beast slowly creeps towards the men. It's a sabre-toothed tiger, man's greatest enemy! Long, sharp fangs hang down either side of its mouth and fearsome claws arm each paw.

# 18 November

No-one but Maku has seen the danger. Maku storms down the hillside shrieking and clattering over stones, making as much noise as possible. The mammoth breaks through the circle of startled men and escapes. Maku's father is about to yell at him when someone spots the tiger. The men attack, throwing their spears and scaring it away. Maku is swept up into his father's arms. He has saved the day. His father is so pleased that he decides to let Maku come along on the next hunt as a lookout. Maku is very proud and vows to be the best lookout ever.

# 19 November

## The Old Lighthouse

Lenny lighthouse was once a very handsome and important building. He was built over two hundred years ago on an outcrop of rock by the sea, alongside a busy shipping lane. His job was to warn ships of the dangerous rocks hiding beneath the water. But as the years went by, ships sailed different routes and Lenny was no longer needed.

# 20 November

Today, Lenny is just a worn out shell. His paint is peeling and all his windows are broken. He hasn't seen anyone for ages. But this morning, Lenny's rock is buzzing with workmen and traffic. He is given a new coat of paint. The lamp, windows and doors are replaced and a large sign is screwed into his wall. It says this is a site of historical interest. Fantastic! Lenny will have lots of visitors and never be lonely again.

# 21 November

## The Sleep Over Party

Tonight, Hannah is having a 'sleep over' party with her three best friends, Michelle, Rosie and Alice. The three girls arrive at Hannah's house at five o'clock and rush upstairs to lock themselves in Hannah's bedroom. They have a list of 'THINGS TO DO'.

First they wash their hair and pin it up in Hannah's mum's pink rollers.

 # 22 November

While their hair is drying, they experiment with the odd bits of make-up that Rosie's mum has donated to the sleep over. The lipstick proves to be particularly difficult! The girls have all brought their favourite party clothes and every bit of jewellery they can find. These go on next. Soon it is time to take the rollers out.

'WOW!' gasps Hannah, as she unravels Alice's hair. 'Now that's what I call curly!'

# 23 November

Alice's hair is an explosion of curls. The friends have a last look in the mirror and then they're ready to party.

First the pizza arrives, thanks to Mum, who is trying very hard to hide a smile. Dad gets the film ready and then they shut the door behind them and leave the girls to enjoy the rest of their sleep over party.

After the film and pizza, the girls roll out their sleeping bags on the bedroom floor.

# 24 November

No sleeping in beds tonight! In fact, no sleeping anywhere really, because the girls end up chatting throughout the night, despite Dad's repeated taps on the wall! The next morning, the girls come down for breakfast yawning and bleary eyed. Mum smiles at them and says, 'I don't know why it's called a sleep-over, when you try to stay awake all night! It's a good job it only happens occasionally. The girls have had a lovely time, but they can't help but agree!

## A Different Sort of Trunk

The elephant family are moving house. Mummy tells Eddie to pack his trunk before the removal men arrive. Eddie finds a stack of boxes, packing cases, bags and suitcases in the attic. He grabs a small one and lays it on his bed. But HOW is he supposed to pack his trunk? When he closes the lid his trunk gets caught!

WHY must he pack his trunk? It's a very useful thing to have. He can unscrew bottle tops with it, feed himself with it, carry things with it - in fact, he'd be totally lost without it!

Downstairs Mummy and Daddy are helping the removal men pack everything into the van.

'Have you packed that trunk yet, Eddie?' asks Mummy. She hears a muffled trumpeting noise from upstairs.

 **27 November**

Moments later, Eddie struggles downstairs with his trunk trapped in the suitcase. Mummy immediately sees Eddie's mistake and bursts out laughing. 'I meant the packing case type of trunk, you silly sausage!' she chuckles, as she opens the lid and rubs Eddie's sore nose. 'Phew! That's a relief,' grins Eddie.

**28 November**

### Roger Rocket's Maiden Voyage

Roger Rocket is training to be a qualified space rocket and today is his first flight into space. He takes a deep breath and begins the countdown: '5,4,3,2,1 - we have lift off!' Roger's engine explodes into life and he streaks up into the clouds. He heads towards the moon marvelling at the shining stars all around him. He orbits the moon twice before Command Centre orders him back to earth. The first flight is a success and Roger is already planning his next one. It may be to Mars, or perhaps even further. Roger can't wait!

# 29 November

## My New Baby Sister

My mummy has a new baby and Daddy and I are going to the hospital to see her. I have made a card with a big, red heart on it for Mummy and I'm giving my very best dolly to my little sister. Daddy is taking Mummy some of her favourite flowers.

Look! There's Mummy in the bed by the big window. She's cuddling the baby. I didn't know she would be this tiny. She's even smaller than my best dolly!

# 30 November

I sit on the bed next to Mummy and she shows me how to hold the baby. She has a wrinkled little face and blue eyes, and fingers and toes which are soooo small and soooo cute. I say to Mummy and Daddy, 'We should call her Tina, because she's so tiny.'

Mummy and Daddy like the name very much, so Tina is what she's called and I think she's the best little sister in the world!

# 1 December

## Little Angel

Angela is a happy little angel. She lives in Heaven with angels from every country in the world. It's a wonderful place, full of kindness and love, where everyone is content, nothing bad ever happens and the sun always shines. Like all angels, Angela hears prayers from people on earth and wants to do her best to cheer them up.

# 2 December

When Angela hears a prayer she blows a kiss and sends it high into the night sky, where it turns into a shooting star. If you look out of your window tonight you might be lucky enough to see one racing through the sky. People who see shooting stars always feel more cheerful. No matter what's happened, it's bound to make you smile.

# 3 December

## Sally's Secret Passage

Sally Shrew scurries through the wood, leaping over gnarled tree roots and crispy, dried leaves, which swirl around in gusts of chilly December wind. She must reach Aunt Shirley's nest before night-time, because it's too dangerous to travel in the dark when owls and foxes like to hunt. Sally is in such a hurry that she doesn't see the big ginger cat quietly stalking her.

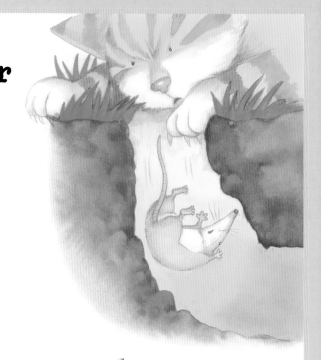

# 4 December

She only realises what's happening when a dark shadow falls over her. Suddenly the cat pounces and Sally veers to her left to avoid being caught in the sharp claws. The chase is on and the cat is much faster than Sally. But Sally swerves left and right, dodging low branches, which slows the cat down. She rounds an oak tree, stumbles over loose pebbles and finds herself tumbling down a deep hole in the ground.

# 5 December

Sally rolls head over heels into a warm, furry body in a nest of straw. Sally has fallen into Rocky Rabbit's burrow. Rocky dusts Sally down and glares up the tunnel at the ginger cat. Luckily, the cat is far too big to squeeze down the tunnel, but his paws claw dangerously at the entrance as he tries to reach them. Sally's safe here, but she's worried that there's no way out!

# 6 December

Rocky isn't at all bothered. While the cat spits and claws at the entrance, Rocky digs another passage in the opposite direction. It's a very long passage and when Rocky finally comes up to the surface, Sally sees that she is right next to Aunt Shirley's nest. Fantastic! Rocky is happy for Sally to use his burrow whenever she likes. And that big ginger cat never did work out how Sally disappeared. I bet he's still prowling around outside Rocky's burrow now!

## Fish in a Fix!

In the warm, sun-drenched waters of the Caribbean Sea is a beautiful coral reef. It looks like an underwater garden, but instead of flowers it is covered in pretty coloured anemones, starfish, plants and sponges. Lots of exotic fish live amongst the coral, like Peter Puffer fish who is playing hide and seek with Lily Lobster, Suki Squid and Pippa Pipefish. Suddenly, a huge shadow slides over the coral blocking out the sunlight.

Panic hits the reef and shoals of fish dive for cover as Grumpy the Shark glides lazily toward them. Grumpy casts a hungry eye over the darting fish, then turns his attention to Peter and his friends who are too terrified to move. Suddenly, Grumpy lunges at them and they all rush to hide in the reef. Lily and Suki find holes at the bottom of the coral. Pippa, being long and thin, squeezes into a narrow crevice and Peter squashes into another cavity.

# 9 December

When puffer fish are afraid, they stick out their spikes and puff themselves up to become twice their normal size. Peter is now so big that he's jammed in tight and cannot move. Grumpy circles the hiding places trying to find a way to catch the fish. Each time he gets too close to Lily Lobster, she nips his nose with her powerful pincers. Each time he gets too close to Suki Squid, she squirts clouds of ink at him.

# 10 December

Grumpy thinks Pippa Pipefish is far too small to be worth eating so he turns to Peter. But there is no way Grumpy can prise Peter out of his hole. Eventually he gives up and swims away. Peter calls for help. Lily and Suki don't know how to rescue him but Pippa Pipefish comes to the rescue. Her long thin body fits easily into the hole. She gives Peter a big push and out he pops. They swim away from Grumpy's territory and have fun playing hide and seek until bedtime.

# 11 December

## The Magical Oak

A long, long time ago there was an enchanted wood, which grew magic oak trees. These special trees could move from wood to wood, disappearing and reappearing as they wished. If you were lucky enough to come across one of these special trees, you would see a small door at the base of the trunk, just big enough to squeeze through if you were a small child. Each door would allow you to visit Fairyland for just one hour. And best of all you would be invisible!

# 12 December

When Josh and Megan's family rent a weekend holiday cottage, the children find a magic oak tree at the bottom of their garden. Megan soon spots the tiny door and Josh pushes it open. Inside it's not dark at all. Bright sunshine streams out of the tree. Josh pokes his head in further and sees green hills and pretty flowers. He just can't resist squeezing all the way through the door and Megan soon follows him.

# 13 December

They decide to explore this amazing place. Fluttering down the lane are two pretty fairies and further along the children come across other fairy folk going about their business. No one pays them any attention and Megan and Josh soon realise they are invisible in this fairy world. They pass toadstool houses, tiny castles, elves and sprites riding colourful dragonflies andbutterflies.

# 14 December

The lane takes them in a large circle and one hour later they find themselves back at the little door. They can hear Dad calling them in for lunch. When they tell Mum and Dad about their adventure, they don't believe them so they decide to show their parents the door. The tree has gone! Mum and Dad smile and go back into the cottage, leaving Megan and Josh wondering if it was all just a dream. Suddenly, on a puff of wind, an elf sails by on a dragonfly and disappears into the wood. The children smile. Now they know it really did happen.

# 15 December

## Bertie Beetle's New Home

Bertie is moving to a new home and he tells Eddie Earwig all about it as he packs his cases. 'It has two rooms, a fantastic garden, a shared swimming pool and as much food as it's possible to eat,' he boasts. 'Why don't you move in with me?' It sounds too good to be true, thinks Eddie! But Bertie is not exaggerating. As they scuttle around the pantry door and climb up a food cupboard, Bertie points out his new home.

# 16 December

It's a small, but attractive sweet tin with two sections, tucked almost out of sight, behind large jars and tins of food. The sweet tin has magnificent views over the garden, (a collection of potted plants), and the swimming pool, (the dog's water bowl), currently being used by their neighbour, Sammy Spider. Eddie has to agree that it's far superior to the old property in the cellar and immediately decides to move in. Bertie and Eddie will be very happy in their new house (until the cleaning lady comes on Thursday!).

# 17 December

## Opposites

Mrs Boylan tells her class that today's lesson is about opposites. The children all split into pairs and their classmates have to guess which opposites they have chosen. Kiran and Jahan are first. This one is easy and everyone raises their hands. Kiran is tall and Jahan is small. Monica and Erica are next. This is easy too. Monica is sitting down and Erica is standing up. Oliver and Lee stand by the door. Oliver is inside the classroom and Lee is outside.

# 18 December

Amelia's desk lid is open and Amanda's is closed. Philip walks backwards and Rodney forwards. Jilly's shoes are dirty and Daisy's are clean. Lily holds her hands up high and Eva holds hers down low. Everyone's opposites have been guessed, apart from Tim and Tom's. They are identical twins and they both sit at their desk with their pencils and exercise books. The children are puzzled. No-one guesses the answer so Tim tells them that he is right handed and Tom is left handed. That was a hard one!

# 19 December

## What Is A Snowflake?

Paula the Polar Bear lives near the North Pole, where snow covers everything. Paula loves the snow and wants to know more about it. Daddy Bear tells Paula that each snowflake is made of lots of tiny ice crystals and each crystal has six sides. Dad draws three shapes in the snow. Paula recognises a triangle with three sides and a square with four sides. Dad says the one with six sides is a hexagon.

Paula spends hours drawing shapes in the snow until more snow falls from the sky and covers up all her patterns. Then Paula bounds away to build a big snowman with her brothers.

# 20 December

## The Strange Little Horse

A herd of beautiful horses live wild in the forest. Trudging alone through the trees is a little foal who has lost his mother and wants to join the herd. The other horses make fun of the little foal because he has a strange bump in the middle of his head, and two more on his back. They don't want another mouth to feed so the foal has to leave.

## 21 December

The foal spends the winter in the barn of a kind farmer. When spring arrives, the little foal has grown tall and strong. The bump on his head is a spiral horn and the bumps on his back are a pair of magnificent wings! He's not a horse at all, he's a beautiful, white unicorn. He spreads his wings and flies into the sky in search of other unicorns. As he rises above the clouds he sees hundreds of them flying towards him.

## 22 December

At the front of the herd he sees his mother. She's been searching for him for months, ever since she lost him in a blizzard. Everyone is so happy to see him. They swoop over the wild horses in the forest and he neighs loudly to get their attention. They wave back, not recognising him, but he doesn't mind. He's just so happy because he's back where he belongs.

# 23 December

## The Christmas Tree

For as long as the fir tree can remember, he has been dug up once a year, taken inside and decorated with baubles for Christmas. Then he has been replanted in the New Year. The fir tree has grown tall and strong over the years and knows he will not fit in the house this Christmas. He fears he will be cut down and thrown away, or chopped up for firewood! When the man arrives carrying a big box, the tree trembles with fear. But when the man pulls out rows of outdoor Christmas lights, he's delighted. Now he's the most handsome tree in the garden.

# 24 December

## It's Christmas!

It's Christmas Eve and there is great excitement in the Harper household, as they prepare for the big day. Kate and John lay the table, Dad peels the vegetables and Mum is tidying and vacuuming the house. Kate and John have written to Santa Claus and can't wait to see what presents he has for them. The children leave a bag of carrots, a glass of milk and mince pies by the fireplace. Then they run upstairs to bed. By nine o'clock they are fast asleep. In the early hours of Christmas morning, Santa's sleigh lands gently on the Harper's roof.

# 25 December

Although the chimney is a tight fit for Santa, he manages to squeeze down with a big sack of toys. He checks his list before digging around for a long, wide, red parcel for John and a smaller, softer parcel tied with pink ribbon for Kate. Then Santa quickly eats the mince pie and drinks the milk, before disappearing back up the chimney with the carrots. The children are up early and wake Mum and Dad. There are lots of presents for everyone downstairs, but John heads straight for the long, wide, red parcel.

He rips off the paper and is delighted to find a shiny new skateboard. Kate gets a beautiful ballerina's outfit and wears it all day. Grandparents, Aunts, Uncles and friends come and go all day. Everyone has a lovely time and eats far too much!

Santa has had a busy day too. After delivering all the presents, he flies home and has his own Christmas party with the reindeer and all the elves. Everyone will sleep well tonight after such a busy time. Santa thinks it's a good job Christmas only comes once a year!

# 26 December

## Old Grandad Tortoise

No one knows how old Grandad Tortoise is. Some say one hundred years old and some say two hundred. Grandad isn't too sure either, but each year on his birthday he asks the youngest member of his family to scratch another line on his shell. None of the other tortoises can guess his age properly because they can only count to ten.

# 27 December

Grandad is the only one able to count higher, but even with a neck as long as his, he is still unable to see all of his shell. Then Grandad has a brilliant idea. He asks each member of the family to count off ten scratches, circle them with a pen, so no-one else counts them, and then stand to one side.

# 28 December

Everyone follows Grandad's instructions and soon twelve tortoises have each counted ten scratches. So all Grandad has to do is multiply ten by twelve. Now everyone knows that tortoises do everything VERY slowly, so after a while the other tortoises begin to drift away and leave Grandad to his calculations.

# 29 December

December passes, along with many more months and years, before Grandad finally works out that he is one hundred and twenty years old! WOW! Clever old Grandad! (Better not tell him that eight years have passed since he started adding up, we don't want him to start all over again, do we?)

# 30 December

## Silly Nita

Nita lives in the snowy Arctic. She shares her igloo home with her mum, dad and baby brother. Furs, blankets and a small fire keep the igloo nice and warm, but Nita thinks a bigger fire would be much cosier. One day, before they all leave on a hunting trip, Nita secretly builds up the fire. She thinks it will be lovely and warm when they return.

# 31 December

The fire is a bit too warm for the icy igloo and the walls soon start to melt. When the family return, the igloo has gone and all that is left is a big puddle of water. Nita is very sorry and wants to help build another igloo. It takes hours to carve out more big blocks of ice, but Nita works twice as hard as Mum and Dad to make up for her silly mistake.

By bedtime the igloo is ready and everyone crawls under their furs and blankets and has a VERY long sleep.